D1178784

The Easy-care Garden

Published by
The Reader's Digest Association Limited
London ▪ New York ▪ Sydney ▪ Montreal

The
Easy-care
Garden

Expert advice on looking after a low-maintenance garden

CONTENTS

Easy-care basics

Around the garden

A–Z of easy-care plants

Introduction

We all live at a frantic pace these days and there seems to be little time left in which to simply relax. Gardening, however, can be the ideal way to unwind and needn't take up every spare moment. Follow the time-saving guidelines in this book and you can enjoy a beautiful garden that will be an oasis of calm in your busy life.

Most of us enjoy doing some work in our gardens but wouldn't want to spend all our spare time on back-breaking chores. The more features you have in your garden – such as formal lawns, beds and borders, ornamental ponds, rockeries or vegetable plots – the more jobs you will have. However, there are techniques that can help to reduce your workload and prevent you becoming a slave to your garden. And if you limit the number of features – for example, to a lawn surrounded by shrubs or a patio filled with containers – you can cut down on the number of jobs you need to do.

There are always going to be some garden tasks that you can't avoid, but if you're prepared to put in a little effort you can reap the rewards later. For example, a few hours spent digging over a flower bed or vegetable patch will ensure the soil is perfect and that your plants will thrive. Spend a little time spreading mulches over your garden and you can inhibit weeds and condition the soil at the same time. And if you pick plants that require little care or attention then you can simply sit back and watch your garden grow!

This book will show you the most useful labour-saving techniques you'll ever need, with plenty of hints and tips on how to maintain – and enjoy – an easy-care garden.

Easy-care
basics

Getting to know your soil

Not all soil is the same and the type in your garden will determine what kind of plants you will be able to grow. Although you can go a long way towards improving the soil, you will reduce your hard work by choosing plants that suit the natural conditions in your garden.

Look at what grows naturally in your garden – this can tell you something about your soil. Dry, sunny slopes, for example, suit entirely different plants than those from damp, nutrient-rich hollows; plants that thrive in loose, friable soil differ from those best suited to heavy clay. When you buy a plant, check the label to see what type of soil it prefers. Although you can change your soil's composition to a degree, picking plants suited to your garden will give you a greater chance of success.

Start by finding out what type of soil you have. Try a quick analysis by cutting out wedges of earth with a spade and looking at them closely: crumbly, sandy soils are normally light coloured; friable, humus-rich soils are dark; and light-coloured soils that stick to the spade are clay. Home soil-testing kits are available from DIY stores and garden centres. Remember to take samples from different locations around the garden.

Touching and smelling the soil gives further clues. Sandy soil with a low clay content crumbles easily and humus-rich soil smells of mushrooms. Clay soils are malleable and sticky when wet. The ideal garden topsoil consists of one third sand, one third clay and one third humus. Working in more of what your particular soil needs will improve the balance.

Light and heavy soils

Light soils drain freely because of their high sand content, and are easy to cultivate. They warm up quickly in spring and are well aerated. However, they do not hold water or nutrients well and dry out quickly. Heavy soils have a high clay content. They are dense, poorly aerated, and difficult to work. They tend to hold water and form clumps.

They are also slow to warm up in spring. On the plus side, they retain water and nutrients well. Most plants like conditions somewhere in between. Ideally, soil should be easy to dig, well aerated, able to retain moisture and fairly rich in nutrients.

Soil improvement

If your soil is heavy, dig it over thoroughly or turn over with a rotavator. Remove large stones and weeds, and then add sand, compost or both to improve and enrich the soil. Spread these over the surface and work into the top layer by digging and hoeing. Level off the surface and the ground is ready to be sown with seeds or planted.

Enrich very sandy soil with bulky organic matter such as well-rotted horse manure. Particularly poor soils can be fertilised by working in blood, fish and bone – at a rate of 50–100g per square metre – in addition to compost. Good soil preparation at the outset will save a lot of time and effort later. Once the soil is planted, roots and organisms living in the soil will keep it loose.

Acid, alkaline or neutral?

As well as understanding your soil type, you need to know its pH-value; this indicates whether a soil is alkaline, neutral or acidic. If more nutrients are leached from soil than are added to it, then the soil will be acidic. Acid rain compounds the process and leads to a disruption in the vital transportation of ions in the soil. This, in turn, causes a delay in the mineralisation process, locking up nutrients that plants need.

The most common soil deficiencies are calcium and magnesium, and these can be spotted easily by characteristic leaf changes in many plants. Adding mineral supplements

The right soil for the right plant

Planting	Nutrient supplements	Action
On sandy soils		
Trees	Lots of compost (1:1)	Mix in the planting hole
Specimen shrubs; vegetables	Compost (1:2)	Rake in or mulch
Lawns	A little compost (1:4)	Rake in
Natural garden; grass	Unnecessary	None
Shrubs	A little compost (1:3)	Rake in or mulch
Dwarf trees or shrubs	A little compost (1:3)	Dig in, mulch or add to planting hole
On clay soils		
Trees	Small amount of compost (1:4 to 1:3)	Mix into planting hole
Specimen shrubs; vegetables	A little sand (1:3) and some compost (1:3)	Rake or dig in
Lawn	A little sand (1:3)	Dig in before laying or sowing
Natural garden; grass	Lots of sand (1:1)	Rake or dig in
Shrubs	A little sand (1:3)	Dig in or mulch
Dwarf trees	Small amount of compost	Dig in or add to planting hole
On humus-rich soils		
Trees	None	None
Specimen shrubs; vegetables	None	None
Lawn	Sand (1:1)	Rake in
Natural garden; grass	Lots of sand (3:1)	Rake in
Shrubs	A little sand (1:3)	Dig or rake in
Dwarf trees	A little sand (1:3)	Dig or rake in, or add to planting hole

such as calcium (contained in mushroom compost, for example) or calcium-rich ground rock or even compost will soon replenish the soil. Working in lime also helps, although this will make the soil alkaline and unsuitable for heathers, azaleas and other acid-loving plants.

TIP To prevent your precious topsoil washing away in the next heavy downpour, simulate a natural top layer with a covering of mulch. Use an organic mulch such as leaf mould or bark chippings (see Basic Care: Mulching, page 16). This will also protect the topsoil from severe changes in temperature.

12 Situation and climate

Different plants need different situations in the garden: some prefer sun over shade, while others need protection from cold weather or shelter from harsh winds. Take conditions and climate in your garden into account when choosing or siting plants and you will save time later.

There are plants that like full sun and plants that like full shade, with plenty in between the two extremes. You need to understand where these areas are in your garden when deciding where to position plants. Shadows cast over your garden will alter dramatically over the course of a year and even throughout the course of the day as the sun moves across the sky. Take such shadows into account and it will save you the time and effort of relocating plants or garden features because they are in the wrong place.

If you have lived in your home for a while, you will already be familiar with areas of sun and shade in your garden, and how these differ as the seasons change. If you have a new garden, draw up a plan of your site and note areas of full sun and shade. Take account of any existing walls, screens and hedges as these will provide effective protection for plants.

Hot and cold

The height of the sun in the sky also determines temperatures in the garden. The higher the sun, the more intense the heat. At ground level, this warmth can be either stored or reflected. Dark paving, for example, absorbs heat and also heats the area around it, creating a warmer micro-climate on the patio than in the surrounding garden. Pale, light-coloured wood and porous stone, on the other hand, scarcely heat up at all. Consider these factors when positioning plants, particularly those growing in containers.

Frost pockets are common in some parts of the country and may be a problem in your garden. If you are planting in an area prone to hard winters, consider the frost tolerance of the plants you choose. Young trees are less frost tolerant, so saplings should be protected. Evergreens are less susceptible to frost, but can dry out during sunny periods

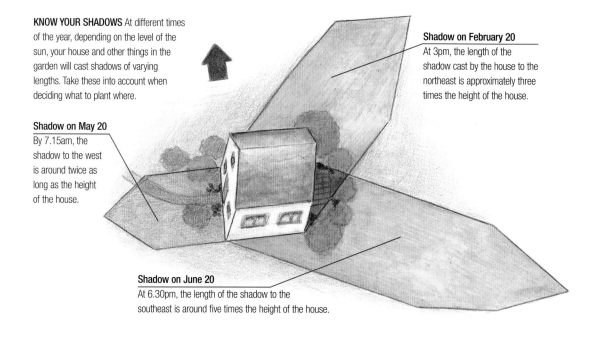

KNOW YOUR SHADOWS At different times of the year, depending on the level of the sun, your house and other things in the garden will cast shadows of varying lengths. Take these into account when deciding what to plant where.

Shadow on February 20
At 3pm, the length of the shadow cast by the house to the northeast is approximately three times the height of the house.

Shadow on May 20
By 7.15am, the shadow to the west is around twice as long as the height of the house.

Shadow on June 20
At 6.30pm, the length of the shadow to the southeast is around five times the height of the house.

in winter; they are unable to draw water out of the frozen earth yet continue to lose moisture through their leaves.

You also need to consider rainfall levels in your area. Even if you don't mind regular watering, there is no point trying to create a damp garden in a region prone to dry, hot summers. In damp areas, pick plants that relish a boggy site and avoid those that react adversely to too much rain, developing problems such as root rot.

Plants can give you clues as to the situations they prefer. Moisture-loving plants generally have broad, tender leaves, while shade-loving varieties tend to have dark green, glossy leaves. Sun lovers often have narrow silvery or hairy leaves. Plants that dislike wind grow low in height; light-hungry varieties strain upwards towards the sunlight. Look around at wild plants that grow well in and near your garden and try to mimic their characteristics when choosing cultivated plants. This will help you pick plants that thrive with little intervention.

Trees and shrubs

Large trees and bushes can exert an important influence on the climate and soil in their immediate environment. Mature trees not only cast shade, but are greedy feeders on the nutrients in your soil. Shallow-rooted trees, in particular, will also suck up a large proportion of the moisture in the ground and can deprive other nearby plants of essential water. Leave autumn foliage where it falls; this will rot down and supply the soil with nutrients as well as keeping in moisture. The warmth given off by the decomposing leaves will also provide a winter habitat for beneficial wildlife.

Slender trees cast narrower shadows than spreading ones, and it is darker under a dense canopy than under a light one. Moisture levels under trees vary considerably: light canopies allow rain through close to the trunk, whereas rain only penetrates at the very edge of a dense

Winter frosts leave many garden plants unharmed and can give some a new charm; the feathery fronds of grasses rimed with frost add interest in a season when many gardens are bare.

canopy. Where the ground is moist, the root system will develop close to the surface; under a dense canopy, roots will penetrate deeper into the soil in search of water.

TIP Computer garden-planning software can help to predict shadow patterns through the year. Alternatively, put stakes in the ground where you plan to plant large shrubs or trees and use them to help you to envisage the shadows that the future plants will cast.

14 Basic care: Composting

Compost is invaluable if you want to improve your soil and give your plants a healthy start in life. It's simple and satisfying to make your own from garden and kitchen waste. Using it will help save time and money, and benefit both your garden and the environment.

A cross-section of the ideal compost heap reveals different layers, with well-rotted compost at the bottom and fresh waste at the top.

Compost is essential if you want to improve the quality of your soil: you can add it to light, sandy soils to increase nutrients and to heavy soils to assist drainage. To ensure a healthy future for a new plant, dig compost into the planting hole.

It's easy to make your own; all you need is a suitable container and a sheltered spot in semi-shade. The container you choose depends largely on what sort of material your garden accumulates, your compost requirements and which techniques you use to maintain the garden. If, for example, you use all your grass cuttings for mulch, sweep all the leaves under the hedge and heap any chopped wood into piles, all you will need, even if you have a large garden, is a thermo-composter for kitchen waste. If, on the other hand, you plan to compost all your garden waste and use a lot of matured compost, you will need more than one container and will probably have to give over more of your garden to compost making.

Which container?

Compost bins are available as both open or closed containers. Open composters (often sold as self-assembly kits) are either made entirely of wood or have metal corner struts and slatted wood sides, or sides made of

Nitrogen providers

Good sources of nitrogen for the compost heap are: kitchen waste, grass clippings, animal manure and nettles.

non-perishable recycled plastic. You can construct your own open composter, either using bricks with holes in them or incorporating a gap under the base of the construction to allow air to reach the compost. Wire containers are particularly airy but do not retain the heat produced by the rotting compost. They are best suited to composting grass cuttings and leaves. Once the compost is well rotted, it can be reached simply by lifting the wire frame from the heap. Some form of opening at the base must be included in all other containers in order for easy access to the mature compost.

Closed compost bins retain heat and moisture well. The composting process is fastest in insulated thermo-composters, which are ideal for composting kitchen waste and small amounts of organic material, though if the raw materials you put in are too wet, the contents may rot.

These kinds of bins can be unattractive, but you can screen them from view – or buy a good-looking bin, such as one that looks like a beehive. If you plan to compost large quantities of leaves, grass cuttings and shredded twigs, you will need additional compost containers.

Compost materials

In the compost heap organic materials are broken down by small organisms and are eventually absorbed by fungi and bacteria. For this, they need warmth, air and moisture. The raw materials composted must also have the correct balance of carbon and nitrogen (approximately 30:1) for the compost to rot down properly. Wet, green materials tend to provide nitrogen and dry, brown ones, carbon. You can keep the process going in summer by watering the compost – but if it gets too wet or too tightly packed, it will be deprived of air.

A compost heap should stand on the soil to encourage earthworms to work their way in. The bottom section can consist of a 20cm thick layer of coarse materials such as the

Compost containers

Bottomless wire containers are unobtrusive, light to move and open. They are ideal for large quantities of leaves, which decompose slowly.

Many wooden composters look attractive. The front section should be easy to open for removing the rotted compost.

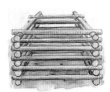

Sealed compost bins should have an adequate supply of air holes in the base and side walls.

When is it ready?

Traditionally, compost was left to rot for two to three years before being used in the garden. Current thinking accepts that a well-constructed compost heap can be ready in as little as 9–12 months, even if all the organic material hasn't completely decomposed.

hard stems of shrubs or coarsely shredded branches, followed by further layers of various organic materials. Try to alternate layers of nitrogen-rich and nitrogen-poor materials. Layers of dry and wet, and coarse and fine material should be alternated, too. Restrict the kitchen waste you use to raw vegetable and fruit waste – cooked leftovers may attract vermin. And never put rooted weeds or their seeds in your compost; many survive the high temperatures of a compost heap and will regrow when you spread the compost on the soil.

Mulching your garden is a great time-saving way to suppress weeds and to feed your soil. A layer of mulch spread around your plants will prevent unwanted weeds growing and will, in the case of organic material, eventually rot down into the soil.

Annual weeds complete their life cycle in one year, propagating by seed and then fading. They are fast growing and invasive, and like exposed soil in well-cultivated beds. Laying a mulch can inhibit germination: the mulch can be either organic, such as lawn clippings or leaf mould, which will decompose; or inorganic, such as plastic sheeting or stone, which will not rot. Choose the right type of mulch for the plants in the bed; for example, do not use leaf mould, which is rich in calcium, in a bed of acid-loving plants.

In a mulched bed without any open soil, many self-seeding plants will also be unable to spread. Choose a mulch that will allow the plants you want to seed and regenerate naturally. In areas of acidic soil, cultivate beds of alkaline, lime-loving plants beneath

Stones or gravel (left) make a good mulch in dry gardens and an attractive setting for low-growing drought-resistant plants.
A mulch sheet is an ideal way to control weeds in a vegetable plot.

Mulches for different situations

Planting	Mulch material	Thickness
Vegetables; herbs	■ Mulch sheets ■ Chopped straw and grass clippings	■ a few mm ■ 3–8cm
Semi to full shade with woodland shrubs and trees	■ Wood chippings, bark mulch, leaves ■ Leaf mould, mulch compost, grass clippings	■ 5–10cm ■ 10–20cm
Mediterranean gravel beds; scented paths	■ Limestone gravel, shale, slate chippings	■ 5–15cm
Sun to semi-shade with shrubs, trees and fruit trees	■ Grass clippings, chopped straw, bark mulch ■ Leaf mould and mulch compost, manure	■ 3–8cm ■ 5–10cm
Dry, sunny open areas with ornamental grasses, low and dwarf shrubs	■ Sand, gravel, stone chippings, chalk ■ Gravel, shale, slate chippings, small pebbles	■ 5–15cm ■ 5–10cm

a thick mulch of limestone chippings that will provide an unappealing environment for the native weeds. An acidic mulch layer will have a similar effect on lime-loving weeds.

Mulching benefits

Not only is mulching a good means of weed control, it also benefits the soil. It helps soil to retain moisture and reduces the amount of watering needed. It also prevents bare earth from 'panning' or forming a hard surface in heavy rain.

Mulched soil will remain light and friable even when a period of heavy rain is followed by hot weather, since water can only seep slowly through the protective layer and will not transform the soil into a solid mass. A good layer of mulch – whether leaf mould, felt, gravel or wood shavings – also insulates the soil against intense heat and cold, providing stable conditions that will benefit any plant.

Using an organic material, such as leaf mould, grass clippings, your own homemade compost or shop-bought bark compost, has the additional advantage of enriching the soil as it rots down, so removing – or at least reducing – the need to fertilise.

Ground-cover plants

The ideal form of low-maintenance soil protection is ground cover. Incorporate a dense covering of this type of plant into your planting scheme from the outset or sow seeds over all areas of bare soil. Bear in mind that ground-cover plants cannot be planted so closely together that the entire surface will be covered right away, so a thick layer of mulch will have to be applied between the young plants until they spread.

Perennial weeds

The best control for perennial weeds is to crowd them out with the plants you do want, as this deprives the weeds of space and light. A mulch can suppress weeds but it will also prevent perennial plants spreading. Digging up weeds may actually encourage growth as most can regenerate from even the tiniest root segment. Since many weeds thrive in heavy soil and lots of sun, a dense planting on well-worked soil is an ideal way to keep them at bay.

TIP Bark mulch can be just as harmful to plants as the weeds themselves: if allowed to touch plant stems it can burn them, and it also locks up nitrogen in the soil.

Plants need water to grow and in areas of low rainfall or at times of drought, you will not be able to rely on rain alone. Ensuring that you have a convenient water supply and an effective irrigation system will save a lot of effort when watering the garden.

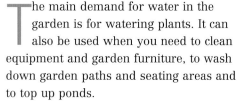

A hose reel equipped with an automatic rewind device is a real boon, saving a lot of time when you come to wind the hose up after watering.
Place a water butt under your drainpipe (below) to gather precious rain water. You can disguise the butt with some attractive climbers.

The main demand for water in the garden is for watering plants. It can also be used when you need to clean equipment and garden furniture, to wash down garden paths and seating areas and to top up ponds.

Since water is increasingly precious, and hosepipe bans are more and more common, most gardens will benefit from the installation of a water butt to collect rain-water runoff from guttering on the house, shed or garage. Heavy users of water in the garden might consider installing an underground tank to store rainwater, from where it can be pumped up to the surface.

One outside water tap in a garden is very useful, but in a large garden more than one is a real boon. If you want to be able to fill a watering can, a tap installed on an outside wall is convenient, while an outdoor sink is an additional bonus for washing pots, tools and muddy boots.

Automatic watering

A time-saving method of watering is to install an automatic sprinkler or drip irrigation system, but both can be wasteful. Automatic sprinklers are fed by pipes buried underground. Water pressure causes sprinklers to pop up from the lawn or bed when switched on. Drip irrigation systems deliver water through small nozzles attached to a network of small bore pipes held in place by spikes stuck in the ground. Alternatively, seep hoses of plastic or rubber, with small perforations along their entire length, can be laid on the surface of the soil. They allow water to sprinkle or trickle out. Hose timers fitted between an outside tap and hosepipe can be programmed to switch the water on and off.

Buy good quality garden tools and take care with their storage and maintenance to protect your investment. Keep your tools clean and dry and they will stay in top condition. Tools that work well save time and trouble – as does keeping your garden shed well organised.

When there's not enough room in your garage for storing garden tools and equipment, the best solution is a garden shed. A wide range of ready-made sheds is available, from patio storage cupboards to larger walk-in buildings.

The type of shed you choose will depend not only on the number and size of your garden tools but also on how much space is available – and your budget. The door should be high enough for you to be able to enter safely and wide enough for you to get larger pieces of equipment in and out. Ideally, there should be room for shelving, the storage of large containers and any garden equipment such as a lawn mower, strimmer or shredder.

Wherever you keep your tools, make sure that they are sensibly and safely stored. A jumble of tools in a garage or shed is impractical and potentially dangerous. Keep tools clean and well maintained and they will last a lifetime. Fix clamps, hooks and brackets on the walls for long handled tools – hang them with sharp points and cutting edges pointing upwards. Many garden centres and tool suppliers sell ready-made storage units and cupboards designed specifically for garden tools.

Mobile storage

A wheelbarrow is essential for transporting heavy and unwieldy objects. Garden caddies, that can be pulled along behind you, can be loaded up with tools so that everything you need is within easy reach.

Smaller hand tools are best kept in a basket, bucket or trug. Belt holsters are practical for carrying secateurs or a garden knife (never keep bladed tools in a pocket), leaving your hands free for other tasks.

Basic care

Plant or sow

Propagate

March

Dig over flowerbeds and veg plots, adding manure or compost. Mulch round fruit trees.

Plant new bare-rooted trees, pot-grown plants and hardy early-flowering shrubs. Sow early-flowering biennials & hardy annuals.

Divide or transplant early-flowering perennials.

April

Deadhead spring-flowering bulbs. Protect new shoots from slugs and snails.

Plant late-flowering shrubs and hardy annuals. Sow herbs and lettuce (protect lettuce seedlings with fleece).

Take softwood cuttings. Take basal cuttings.

May

Weed and mulch beds. Deadhead regularly. Stake tall-growing plants. Mulch strawberries. Clean ponds, removing algae.

Plant early annuals. Sow perennial seeds. Plant out early veg. Sow beans.

Divide water lilies and other aquatics.

June

Feed and deadhead roses. Cut back spring-flowering perennials to encourage a second show. Stake tall plants. Mulch beds.

Plant out the last annuals. Plant out vegetables.

Take greenwood cuttings. Take soft-tip cuttings of tender perennials.

July

Water new plants thoroughly in periods of drought, especially trees and shrubs. Remove weed and algae from ponds.

Plant clump-forming summer annuals in gaps in the herbaceous border.

Take semi-ripe cuttings. Divide and transplant iris.

August

Stop feeding roses. Cut off seedheads of any plant you do not want to self-seed.

Plant autumn-flowering bulbs and evergreens.

Take cuttings of fuchsias and pelargoniums.

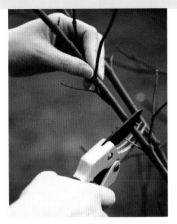

Prune

Prune roses, vigorous shrubs and blackcurrant & gooseberry plants. Thin out late-flowering shrubs. Trim hedges.

Prune early and winter-flowering shrubs, and dwarf and small varieties of trees and shrubs.

Cut back early-flowering container-grown shrubs.

Prune *Prunus* trees when in full growth.

Prune fruit trees after fruit has been harvested.

Remove dead wood from roses (except climbers). Remove dead or damaged branches from fruit trees.

Containers

Clean out empty pots. Increase watering of over-wintered container plants.

Plant up new pots. Gradually harden off new and existing container plants. Re-pot pot-bound plants.

Plant out containers with summer bedding. Remove bulbs from pots, dry and store.

Finish planting up summer pots. Dig up pot-grown spring bulbs, dry off and store.

Apply liquid feed. Water regularly.

Plant winter-flowering heathers and chrysanthemums in pots.

Lawns

First cut of the year. Trim edges. Level out any bumps and hollows, and repair bare patches.

Aerate and feed. Remove thatch and moss. Prepare ground for sowing seed. Sow new lawns and bare patches. Second mowing of year.

Start regular weekly/fortnightly mowing. Avoid mowing areas of naturalised bulbs until foliage has died back.

Mow the lawn when the grass is about 7cm high.

Aerate and feed. Prepare a seedbed for any new lawn areas.

Sow seed for new lawns. Mow weekly and stop any feeding.

Basic care

Plant or sow

Propagate

September

Rake up leaves and add to compost or store for use as mulch.

Plant early-flowering spring bulbs. Sow the seed of hardy annuals.

Take ripewood cuttings. Divide and transplant clump-forming herbs that have grown too big.

October

Dig up any non-hardy bulbs, dry out and store. Cut back summer-flowering perennials.

Plant late-flowering spring bulbs. Plant winter and spring lettuce plants.

Divide and transplant herbaceous perennials.

November

Mulch flowerbeds with leaves. Prepare new beds for spring planting and cover with mulch.

Plant out bare-rooted trees and shrubs. Plant garlic.

Take hardwood cuttings of shrubs, currants and gooseberry bushes.

December

Protect any shrubs of borderline hardiness with horticultural fleece. Plan plantings for the year ahead and order seeds.

Plant herbs in pots to grow on the windowsill. Plant out hedging shrubs if the soil is workable.

Take root cuttings where required and place in a cold frame or greenhouse.

January

Prevent snow breaking the branches of shrubs and trees by shaking it off if it settles. Dig over new beds and leave clods on top to be broken up by frost.

Sow seeds for annuals under glass or on a warm windowsill.

Take hardwood cuttings of climbing plants during mild spells.

February

Cut back ornamental grasses. Order young bedding plants and summer-flowering bulbs.

Sow early carrots and spinach outdoors under cloches. Sow tomato and courgettes under glass or on a warm windowsill.

Take cuttings of pelargoniums for rooting in a propagator.

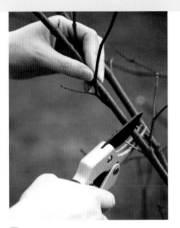

Prune

Cut back summer-fruiting raspberry canes.

Prune any fruit trees where all the fruit has been harvested (but not apples).

Cut back deciduous hedges once they have lost their leaves.

Prune apple trees. Cut back late autumn-flowering shrubs.

Prune trees and climbing plants on frost-free days.

Prune autumn-flowering raspberry canes.

Containers

Plant up pots with spring-flowering plants and bulbs, and set aside in a sheltered spot.

Wrap less hardy plants and their pots in fleece and store in a sheltered place.

Bring tender plants into the conservatory or greenhouse.

Bring winter and spring-flowering containers in under cover during spells of severe weather.

Deadhead any winter-flowering plants.

Empty out and thoroughly clean pots ready for spring planting.

Lawns

Aerate and remove moss. Go round the borders of the lawn with an edging tool.

Reduce mowing to once every two weeks.

Treat waterlogged areas by adding sand and make drainage holes with a fork.

Rake up any last leaves and avoid walking on the grass if frozen or waterlogged.

Mow any areas of rough grass if the weather is dry and fine.

Lift and divide any naturalised snowdrops straight after flowering. Tidy and repair any loose edges.

Around the garden

26 Herbaceous borders

Herbaceous perennials provide colour for every season in the garden. They may die back when winter comes but appear anew the following season. Provided that growing conditions are suitable, these plants require little attention and will give years of pleasure.

A well planned herbaceous border will give long-term structure to your garden. Perennial flowering plants come in many different shapes and sizes. They die back to ground level each autumn, growing back vigorously the following spring and flowering once again. As well as varieties that flower for only a relatively short period each year there are perennials that flower repeatedly throughout the whole summer – the perfect chioce for low-maintenance gardening.

Christmas roses unfurl their flowers while it is still winter, followed in spring by primulas. In spring, too, flowering bulbs such as snowdrops, crocuses, scilla and daffodils brighten the border. Phlox, bellflowers and day lilies provide colour

Drifts of herbaceous perennials interspersed with splashes of annual colour will make an impressive display in any garden.

from July until autumn, when Michaelmas daisies, sedums, chrysanthemums and yellow rudbeckias come into their own.

When early flowering perennials, such as bleeding heart, die back leaving gaps in the border, you can infill with summer bedding (see page 29). Other plants, like hostas and *Heuchera*, have decorative foliage that lasts long beyond flowering.

A display for every garden

Plant herbaceous perennials together in borders according to flowering period, colour and size, so that they produce a pleasing show of blooms throughout the whole year. There are perennials suitable for every type of garden and situation – whether dry, sunny, shady or damp. When designing herbaceous borders, think about the requirements of individual plants. Shade lovers will not thrive alongside sun worshippers, and plants that prefer a dry situation will be susceptible to fungal diseases if planted in a damp location.

Spring or autumn are the best times to plant a herbaceous border. Before you start planting, work a good quality compost or a slow-release fertiliser into the soil to provide vital nutrients. Restrict yourself to a handful of different plants – combining too many different varieties will make the border seem muddled. Place several of the same variety together and group plants by height, putting taller varieties at the back.

A natural look

One of the secrets of creating an attractive herbaceous border is to position the plants so that they appear natural and, at the same time, to make sure that each plant has enough light and space in which to develop. Tall plants such as delphiniums, phlox and foxgloves create focal points and form the framework of the bed. They tower over medium-height varieties such as *Erigeron*, loosestrife and cranesbill, which should be planted further forward in the border. Lower

Support any tall perennials early in the season to prevent them getting damaged or knocked down by heavy rain or strong wind.

growing plants such as lady's mantle or ground-cover plants like creeping phlox and aubretia are ideal for the front of the border, where they can also act as edging to a path or lawn.

Prepare a plan of your border on paper first. Make sure you take into account the light and climate conditions of the bed and the type of soil; this will determine which perennials will thrive in that situation. Then check the planting requirements and final size of your preferred plants before you buy to avoid costly mistakes. Look on the plant label or consult a garden encyclopedia or the directory here (see page 90).

Once you are happy with your plan, mark the outlines of your planting groups on the bed itself using a trickle of sand; curved lines make the planting look more natural. Then stand the plants onto the bed in their pots and move them until you are happy with the arrangement. By and large, tall

Dividing perennials

Perennials should be divided every three to five years. This rejuvenates plants and is also an easy way to propagate them.

1 Begin by lifting the plant to be divided with a garden fork. If the root stock is too hard and compact, first trim it with a spade.

2 Use the blade of the spade or a strong knife to break the clump up, especially if the rootstock is compact.

3 For plants with a loose root system simply pull the roots apart with your hands after lifting.

perennials such as delphiniums and foxgloves should be planted about 50–80cm apart; medium height plants should be around 40–60cm apart and small ones 20–30cm apart.

Buy healthy plants

Check that the plants you buy are free from pests and have strong healthy leaves and roots. Ideally, plant spring and early summer-flowering varieties in autumn and late summer and autumn-flowering varieties in spring – though you can plant pot-grown plants at any time of year if the ground is not frozen and you water them in well. Don't apply any fertiliser in the first few weeks, as too many nutrients will inhibit root development. At six to eight weeks, a slow-release fertiliser will ensure good growth and abundant flower formation. Water borders regularly in hot dry summers, and apply a layer of mulch to stop the ground from drying out.

Herbaceous border care

Catmint and tickseed have long flowering periods, but you can extend the flowering of many other plants by deadheading as soon as the flowers fade. Lady's mantle and cranesbill, for example, will flower again if cut back by about 10cm after their first flowering. Older plants may begin to produce fewer flowers than usual but these can be easily revived by lifting and dividing them. This will also reduce the size of an overgrown plant.

Dividing plants will keep them healthy but it is also a good way to propagate them. After lifting a plant you can divide the clump into two or more, replanting each piece to make more plants. Most plants respond best to division if done in autumn; choose only the strongest and best established plants to divide to ensure healthy new specimens. Some plants do not like being divided – Christmas roses and peonies, for example – so it is a good idea to check before you proceed. When replanting the divisions, make sure you leave plenty of space in between for them to grow into.

Overhauling a border

If you inherit an overgrown herbaceous border you will need to rejuvenate the existing bed before planting out any new specimens. Start by cutting back all existing perennials to give you a better view of the whole bed. Lift individual plants, removing and discarding any weeds tangled in the roots, then divide and set aside. Clear all weeds from the bed, taking care not to leave any roots behind, then dig over to loosen the topsoil. Remove large lumps of soil or stones and work in some compost. Replant the divided perennials in their desired position and add any new plants as required.

When gaps appear in beds and borders, as they do in most gardens from time to time, why not fill them with fast-growing annuals? These plants last just the one season but they are easy to grow from seed. Alternatively, you can buy young specimens, ready to plant out as bedding.

Quick and colourful annuals such as nasturtiums soon fill a border with a profusion of brightly coloured flowers.

When you plant out a new border there will be big bare areas between the various perennials, grasses and shrubs where gaps have been left to allow the plants to grow. Such bare patches are unattractive and, being exposed to the weather, they can lose moisture rapidly on a hot or windy day. The best way to fill such gaps is with summer bedding. Choose unfussy varieties that grow quickly, such as nasturtiums, pot marigolds, alyssum or verbena. You can sow these directly into the ground or, better still, put in growing plants.

Early flowering plants, such as tulips, that die back quickly, can also leave gaps in established borders; pruning might also create gaps. Again, summer bedding plants can come to the rescue. If you want to prevent bedding plants from spreading too much, leave them in their pots and sink them, pots and all, into the ground. In autumn, simply take out the filler plants, or leave them *in situ* over winter and dig the remains into the ground in spring.

Problem areas

In many gardens there are areas where, in spite of every effort, nothing will flourish. Either the ground is too heavy and constantly waterlogged, or it is much too dry and stony. Rather than taking costly and time-consuming measures to improve the soil, put a large container full of colourful bedding plants in the problem spot.

Snails have a passion for bedding plants. Instead of picking off the culprits one by one, drown snails in a beer trap or attract and trap them in old cabbage leaves or empty grapefruit halves. Collect them and put them in your lidded green recycling bin or tip them into a distant hedgerow or some uncultivated ground.

30 Dry borders

In dry situations in full sun the leaves and flowers of many plants can wilt quickly. If your garden has such an area, don't try to change conditions; simply create a natural-looking border with tough drought-resistant plants and you won't have to worry about watering.

On hot, dry summer days, you can easily spot the plants that need little attention and those which will wilt all too quickly unless you water them. Many plants prefer a position in full sun, but few can withstand extreme drought. With hosepipe bans becoming a feature of summer in many parts of the country, why not create a border that needs little or no watering? The best way to do this is to choose a planting scheme that imitates nature.

There are many flowering native or naturalised wild flowers that are attractive enough to earn a place in a garden border and that will even flourish on dry and infertile ground. Red valerian, golden marguerite and sea holly, for example, will flower tirelessly throughout summer and into autumn, attracting bees and butterflies into the garden. In addition, these plants are often resistant to pests and diseases, unlike more highly bred cultivated perennials.

The purple spikes of sage bring vibrant colour to the garden and prove that a dry border need not be dull and dessicated.

Creating a dry border

Most sun-loving plants – such as marguerites and evening primroses – are naturally opportunistic and successfully colonise waste ground on embankments or tips. They love infertile ground and dry places. Mimic these conditions by incorporating sand and gravel into your garden soil to increase its permeability and reduce its fertility; if the pH value of your soil is too acidic, you could add a little lime to compensate.

The ideal situation for a dry border is along the edge of a gravel path or in front of a dry stone wall. Laying gravel or stone chippings between the individual plants adds to the illusion that they are growing from dry and barren ground. The effect will be most successful if you plant in groups of a few varieties, creating drifts of each different type of flower.

Break up the planting with a few clumps of wafting grasses and include a few tall bulbs, such as alliums, to create striking highlights and to prolong the flowering season of the bed.

Don't overwater

Sun-worshipping, drought-tolerant plants have strong, deep root systems to allow them to withstand prolonged dry periods. They find moisture deep in the ground and can easily be overwatered if you add more yourself. They only need regular watering during the first year after planting, to help them to put down strong roots. Once established, only water plants on the rare occasions when drooping leaves and flowers indicate that the plant has dried out.

When choosing drought-resistant plants for the dry border, look out for those with silvery grey leaves, such as the curry plant (*Helichrysum italicum*).

Plants for a border in full sun

Plants	Flowering period/ Flower colour
Golden marguerite (*Anthemis tinctoria*)	June to September; yellow
Mullein (*Verbascum*, different varieties)	July to September; yellow, pink or violet
Globe thistle (*Echinops*)	July to September; blue
Evening primrose (*Oenothera*, different varieties)	June to September; usually yellow
Yarrow (*Achillea*, different varieties)	June to September; red, yellow and white
Gypsophila (different varieties)	May to September, depending on variety; white or pink
Red valerian (*Centranthus ruber*)	May to July, often lasting into autumn; red or pink
Sage (*Salvia*, different varieties)	May to October; shades of pink, purple and blue

Herbaceous perennials that like semi-shaded positions generally require little attention. Plants that would naturally be found along the margins of woodland are ideal if you want to create an easy-care border under a large tree or in areas shaded by walls, hedges or the house.

A semi-shaded corner of the garden enjoys similar conditions to a woodland edge. It is easy and quick to create an attractive, low-maintenance border with plants that are at home in this environment. The results are particularly effective if you put several specimens of the same plant together. They can spread quickly via runners, or by layering or seeding, filling neglected shady areas and flowering after a short time.

Once planted, you can leave the semi-shaded border to look after itself – more or less. All you need to do is some light maintenance – mulching now and again, thinning out plants that are growing too vigorously and watering in dry years.

Brighten up borders

Brightly coloured flowers bring light and colour to shady corners. The slim, radiant white flower spikes of bugbane appear from summer to autumn, depending on the variety. Or try monkshood, campanula or sky blue Jacob's ladder. The flowers of small plants such as *Brunnera* are happiest left undisturbed and need little deadheading. Plants with decorative foliage, such as hostas, are also ideal for semi-shaded borders, while lungwort – which flowers in spring and bears attractive white-flecked leaves until dying back in autumn – will flourish in damp soils.

There are many easy-care groundcover plants suitable for moist, semi-shaded positions, such as creeping Jenny or bugle. However, dry ground can cause problems for many plants growing under shallow-rooted shrubs, and you might want to consider a drip hose irrigation system on such inhospitable territory. You can help by mulching round plants occasionally with leaves, wilted grass cuttings or mushroom compost. Some plants, such as cranesbill and Welsh poppies, will do fine here even without extra watering.

Plants for semi-shade

Plants	Flower colour/Growth habit/Height
Columbine (*Aquilegia vulgaris*)	Violet, blue, pink, white; upright; 50–70cm
Monkshood (*Aconitum*)	Blue; upright; 1–1.5m
Jacob's ladder (*Polemonium*)	Blue; upright; 30–60cm
Bellflower (*Campanula glomerata*)	Violet to lavender, blue or white; bushy; 50–60cm
Lungwort (*Pulmonaria*)	Pink, red, violet, purple, blue or white; bushy; 20–30cm
Common foxglove (*Digitalis purpurea*)	Purple, pink, white; upright; 1–2m
Bugbane (*Cimicifuga*)	White, cream; upright; 60–90cm
Goat's beard (*Aruncus dioicus*)	Creamy-white; spreading; 1–1.2m
Cranesbill (*Geranium sylvaticum*)	Blue to purple, pinkish purple, pink or white; bushy and upright; 50–70cm

Beds that enjoy dappled shade need not be dull; flowering plants like the frothy *Astilbe* and the black-stemmed *Ligularia* thrive here.

34 Shady borders

There are some garden plants that thrive in deep shade – including flowering species. But among some of the best shade lovers are those plants prized for their foliage. You can combine such specimens to create a verdant border that demands little attention – the foliage will even suppress weeds.

Some plants positively flourish in gloomy half-darkness under tree canopies or in the shadows cast by buildings or walls. Such shade lovers prefer moist ground, rich in humus, so if your soil is light, enrich it with leaf mould, compost and manure.

There are many species that will turn a shady place in the garden into an attractive, low-maintenance border. *Rodgersia*, foxgloves and bugbane are tall, upright, undemanding plants that give structure to a shady border. They brighten up shadows with their flowers and their leaves provide striking structural highlights. Position them at the back of the border so that they do not obscure other plants. Use smaller plants such as *Astilbe* or hostas alongside taller specimens as a foil for the more statuesque, structural plants. Fill gaps in the border with ferns, shade-loving grasses and smaller foliage plants. The varied colours and shapes of their leaves will help to bring the whole planting scheme to life.

Liven up with greenery

Deeply shaded areas are easily brightened up with lively foliage plants. For maximum visual appeal, group together a number of

Foliage plants like hostas and ferns can provide a range of different colours and textures that bring life and interest to any shady border.

Plants with good foliage for shady borders

Plants	Foliage	Height
Bergenia, species and varieties	Large, rich green leaves, turning bronze or reddish in autumn	20–60cm
Yellow archangel (*Lamium galeobdolon*)	Serrated yellow leaves with creamy white centres	30–60cm
Hosta, species and varieties	Strikingly veined; many different shades of blue and green with various markings in white or yellow	40–60cm
Spotted dead-nettle (*Lamium maculatum*)	Serrated, mid-green leaves with different and beautiful silver markings	30–60cm
Heuchera, species and varieties	Varying from smooth to wavy; various shades of red, purple and brown according to species; also light green or orange; occasionally finely ruffled	30–60cm
Rodgersia, species and varieties	Deeply veined large leaves; often bronze or red tinged with contrasting coloured veins	60–180cm

plants with leaves of different shapes and colours. Large wide leaves, such as those of the giant *Gunnera*, will enliven large areas and contrast well with tall grasses. The broad, strikingly veined and sometimes variegated leaves of hostas contrast with feathery *Astilbe* and ferns. Fill the foreground with *Bergenia* and lady's mantle or low-growing ground-cover plants like perennial forget-me-nots.

Leave breathing space

If possible, plant shade lovers on cool, cloudy days – newly planted perennials will soon begin to suffer from lack of water in hot weather. Before planting the border, set out plants in their pots on the prepared area. Allow enough space between ferns and grasses so their shapes can be fully appreciated. Winter-hardy ferns which keep their fronds until spring provide a splendid contrast to spring-flowering bulbs like snowdrops and crocuses.

Give plenty of space to flowering plants like *Astrantia* and Solomon's seal. These take up a lot of room when fully grown, but achieve their full potential only when allowed to grow freely – so resist thinning them out too soon.

Water new plants thoroughly after planting and during the first few weeks to encourage root development. Established plants, however, need watering only during long dry spells – although if the bed is in the dry shade of a wall, your plants will probably need more regular watering. If there are no ground-cover plants, apply a layer of mulch to help prevent the soil from drying out, retain warmth and discourage weeds. Otherwise, all you need to do is to remove dead stems or faded flowers from time to time and thin out any plants that have spread too much after a few years.

Over time, plants should spread to fill gaps and cover the ground completely. There will then be no need to mulch, and your border will, by and large, look after itself. You can also leave the dead foliage from surrounding shrubs and trees on the ground in autumn to form a natural mulch.

36 Flowering bulbs

Spring-flowering bulbs can bring colour to the garden while many other plants still lie dormant. Those that bloom later in the year are an ideal way to bridge gaps in flowering. Many bulbs can be simply planted and then forgotten – until the new shoots remind you of their presence.

Drifts of spring-flowering crocuses naturalised in grass bring a welcome show of colour after the dark days of winter.

When planting bulbs, corms and tubers make sure they are free from damage, firm when you squeeze them and that the roots have not begun to grow. Always plant bulbs as soon as possible after buying them.

Ideally, plant spring-flowering bulbs and tubers in autumn, summer-flowering ones in spring and autumn-flowering ones in summer. Pot-grown bulbous plants can be planted at any time but be gentle with their fragile roots.

Make sure you plant bulbs with the tips pointing upwards and plant two to three times as deep as the height of the bulb – a bit deeper in light sandy soil and slightly less deep in heavy clay. The ideal distance between bulbs is half the mature height, in other words 3–5cm for small species and 30–50cm for the tallest.

Many tuberous plants, such as gladioli and dahlias, are not hardy and can only be planted out after the danger of frost has passed. Once they have finished flowering and the first frosts have blackened the foliage, cut the stems down to about 15cm, lift the tubers and store them upside down in a dry, frost-free place for around three weeks until they dry out. Then store (the right way up) with the tubers buried in sand or sawdust in a cool, dark, frost-free place.

Planting in baskets

Bulbs are most effective when planted in groups. The lower-growing the species, the more plants are needed to create a good effect. Use planting baskets to plant groups of different species very close together. Simply bury the planted baskets up to the rim in the flowerbed and cover with soil. If

Planting bulbs in the lawn

Use a bulb planter (see below) with really large bulbs; for others use the following technique.

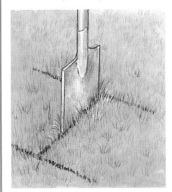

1 Cut an H-shape into the turf with your spade, then cut horizontally underneath the turf and peel back the sides.

2 Now loosen the earth in the exposed patch with a garden fork. Scatter the bulbs over the area and press them in firmly with the growing tip pointing upwards. Replace the turf and press it gently back in place.

you need to lift the bulbs in autumn, you can remove the baskets without damaging either the bulbs or the surrounding plants.

Naturalising bulbs

Flowering bulbs can look vibrant planted in a lawn, though if you mow regularly choose those that bloom outside the mowing season. To ensure a natural-looking planting, scatter bulbs at random over the lawn and plant them where they fall. Using a spade, remove a patch of grass and the

earth beneath it from the lawn. Mix a little of the soil that has been removed with some fertiliser, and put this in the bottom of the hole. Put the bulb on top and cover it with the remaining soil and the patch of grass.

Smaller bulbs are best planted in groups in the lawn. To do this, stick the prongs of a garden fork into the grass and move them back and forth until the holes are wide enough to take the bulbs. Mix soil with some fertiliser and spoon a little into the planting holes. Insert the bulbs and top up with the remaining soil and fertiliser mixture. Once planted, most bulbs will multiply and spread quite happily on their own, often forming fairly large groups after one or two years.

A bulb planter is easy to use; press it into the ground and lift out a plug of soil. Drop the bulb in the hole, then cover with the soil plug.

Care of naturalised bulbs

To ensure that the bulbs you plant provide splashes of colour for years to come:
- deadhead tulips and daffodils on a regular basis as the flowers fade;
- only plant daffodils, tulips and grape hyacinths in lawns that you do not intend to mow until they have finished flowering and have begun to die back;
- with daffodils in particular, don't mow until their foliage begins to yellow, usually six weeks after flowering.

Grass borders

Grass doesn't need to be confined to the lawn – there are many species of ornamental grass available that will add a soft and subtle touch to a border. Plant grasses in the right position and all that most varieties need is a good trim in spring.

Ornamental grasses are surprisingly versatile and come in a wider range of colours than you might at first imagine.

Grasses are easy to look after and great value as they provide year-round interest. They work well whether grown in a group or planted alone as a specimen plant; they can loosen up a formal flowerbed or brighten a dull area. The tallest species, such as pampas grass, are particularly effective as stand-alone plants. Clumps of slightly shorter fountain grass also need plenty of space to show off their beauty, whereas fescue and other low-growing grasses look good in groups. There are grasses for all situations: blue oat grass and switch grass, for example, like dry, sunny positions; sedges and woodrushes require damp humus-rich soil and shade.

Easy-care grasses

Plant grasses in spring when the soil is warming up and drier weather is approaching – those planted in autumn suffer in damp winter weather and may come back only sparsely in spring.

You don't need to feed or water grasses. All that's required is to cut back all the old stems in spring, taking care to avoid young shoots. Low-growing evergreens, such as *Carex comans* 'Frosted Curls', need no clipping at all. If you need to curb vigorous grasses like miscanthus, trim back the roots with a spade. Alternatively, plant them in a bottomless container and sink in the ground; this will restrict the spread.

Winter care

It is easy to protect grasses in severe conditions in winter so they do not rot. Take hold of the clump of grass and gather it together, twisting it rather like hair and tying with twine to prevent cold and wet penetrating the crown of the plant.

A well-planned rockery can be a particularly easy feature to maintain. Once you've created a miniature landscape from different rocks and stones, you can plant it up with some charming species of perennial alpines. Many of these plants are low growing and can quickly form an attractive display.

Rockeries can be an important feature in the garden, displaying low-growing, wide-spreading alpines to best advantage.

Rock gardens work best on a slope – make use of an existing slope or build your own mound. Buy rocks from a DIY store, garden centre or local quarry. It will look more natural if you stick to a single type of rock but vary the sizes. Tufa is a good choice – it's a porous limestone that retains moisture so that plants can grow in cavities in rocks as well as between them.

Building a rock garden

The best time to construct your rock garden is in autumn, planting it up in spring. Choose a sunny, open site with good drainage. If you are building a mound from scratch, use rough chunks of rock, pebbles and rubble to form the basis; take care not to make it too steep. Then add a 10–20cm layer of soil on top. Put the most interesting looking rocks you have on the outside where they will be seen.

Arrange the stones so that they are secure and cannot roll away or slip out of place after heavy rainfall. Lay them flat on their broadest side or embed roughly a third of their volume in the slope. Tipping the rocks back slightly will make them more stable.

Small is beautiful

Choose small perennials that grow little more than 10–20cm in height. Check the flowering season when choosing your plants to make sure that there is always something in bloom. Plant bulbs such as wild tulips or miniature daffodils to flower in the early spring. Many ground-cover plants, like creeping phlox, are spring flowering. Plant low-growing varieties of bellflower and pinks for summer colour, while Edelweiss and gentians will bloom well into autumn. For year-round interest, include some low-growing grasses or even dwarf conifers.

Growing roses

The rich blooms and heady scent of roses make them the stars of the garden in summer. If you give them good growing conditions, they are also easy to maintain. You can plant them in a traditional rose bed or combine with other plants for a less formal border.

True garden stalwarts and perennial favourites, roses provide a magnificent show of beautiful blooms in summer

When you plant a rose in suitable soil, in a good position with enough space and sunlight, it will require little attention and give pleasure for years. And if you choose varieties approved by bodies such as the Royal National Rose Society, these are relatively trouble-free.

Dig a planting hole large enough to take the roots or root ball comfortably; the graft union (the thick nodule at the base of the stem between roots and shoots) needs to sit 2.5cm below ground level. Loosen heavy clay with a fork and improve by adding sand and compost or well-rotted manure. Carefully firm the soil around the newly planted rose and water it in well. Feed roses with a compound or organic fertiliser, first in spring and then once again in summer after the first flush of flowers.

Simple pruning guidelines

Pruning improves flowering – and it is a simple, quick and satisfying job. Always ensure you use sharp secateurs and cut back to healthy wood to an outward facing bud, using a slanting cut.

Prune large-flowering bushes (hybrid tea) and cluster-flowering bushes (floribunda) in winter, but not when it's frosty. Remove weak, diseased, dead and crossing stems. Cut main stems of large-flowering bushes to 20–25cm from ground level and cluster-flowering bushes to 25–45cm.

Prune shrub roses (including species and old-fashioned roses) after flowering. They need little pruning in the first few years, and only a little light pruning as they age. Remove dead, diseased, weak and crossing stems and cut back older wood.

Ground-cover roses require little pruning other than to remove any upright stems; they are meant to provide a thick, colourful carpet. Patio roses also need little pruning, apart from to keep their shape and remove dead and diseased stems. (For ramblers and climbers, see page 42.) You also need to remove suckers – these are shoots from the wild rose that was used as rootstock and they grow out from below the budding union. Such shoots will have the features of the wild rose and if allowed to grow, they can take over from the cultivated one. Uncover the neck of the rootstock and tear off any suckers; if you cut them off they are more likely to regrow.

Pests and diseases

Feeding roses in spring and after flowering helps their resistance, but you should still check them regularly. Many pests can be treated with derris dust or a solution of washing-up liquid. Spray off aphids with a jet of water or pick off and crush with your fingers. Remove diseased leaves from the bush and from the soil – don't leave them lying on the ground. It's best not to plant new roses in an old rose bed, as the soil may be poor in nutrients and contaminated by viruses and fungi.

Pruning roses

- ▥ Cut back the stems of large-flowering bush roses to 20–25cm before new growth starts in early spring and remove dead, damaged and diseased wood at the same time (below, top).
- ▥ Prune shrub roses lightly – at the most back to a third – and remove dead, damaged and diseased wood and any crossing stems (below, bottom).

Large-flowering bush rose

Shrub rose

Year-round rose care

Spring Complete any pruning before new growth starts, but not during frosty conditions. Apply a rose fertiliser. A layer of mulch about 8cm deep, applied around the base of the plant after pruning, helps to suppress weeds and retain moisture.

Summer Inspect regularly for pests and diseases, remove suckers (see above) and deadhead. Water both newly planted and established roses in dry weather. Give a second feed of fertiliser after flowering.

Autumn Plant bare-root roses. Cut back large and cluster-flowering bushes by about one third to prevent wind-rock. Provide winter protection if prolonged harsh weather is forecast.

Winter Shake off thick snow as it can break branches. If severe weather is forecast, heap earth around the base of the plant to protect it. If pruning dormant roses, avoid doing so in frosty weather.

Roses climbing around the door, clambering over an archway or scrambling up an old apple tree look entrancing and add height and interest to the garden. Given a suitable support these ever-popular plants can create a stunning feature in any garden.

A wrought-iron ogee-shaped arch provides the perfect support for *Rosa* 'Santana'.

Climbing and rambling roses offer the gardener the opportunity to surround themselves with colour and scent. They can be trained up and along structures, achieving a magnificent height and spread. A rose-covered bower may take a few years to establish, but it then requires little more than a yearly tidy. You can buy frameworks for training climbing plants in a variety of shapes and materials and a pergola is easy to build. Make sure that whatever structure you choose is stable and strong enough to bear the weight of the climbing plants; if you build an arch or pergola, set it in solid concrete footings.

All climbing plants grow straight up towards the light and the flowers form mainly in the upper sections of the plant. With care you can achieve an even distribution of roses over the lower parts of the support as well as at the top.

Training climbers

To ensure climbing roses give an abundant show of evenly distributed flowers, they should only be allowed to grow in height slowly. It is the horizontal growth that produces the most buds. Bend new pliable side shoots in and around your support before they mature and stiffen and leave firm, upright shoots to flower in the gaps. Tie the shoots in gently with twine in February or March.

There is a difference between climbing and rambling roses but they can share typical features making it hard to distinguish between the two sometimes. Climbers have long, firm, upright shoots ending in large single flowers or clusters of flowers, and most repeat flower from summer to autumn. You can, therefore, produce a second flowering by deadheading regularly, although this will not always be practical on taller specimens. Ramblers have long flexible shoots with clusters of small flowers and usually flower only once in early summer. The display, however, can be particularly abundant and last for several weeks. Both types need to be trained on supports but ramblers are less suitable for growing against walls where the air is frequently still and mildew is, therefore, more likely to develop on the dense growth.

Pruning techniques

Prune climbing roses from late autumn to early spring, before growth resumes but do not prune during the first year after planting. After that, prune the side shoots only, cutting each back by about two-thirds.

Prune old climbing roses to coax new growth on lower shoots. Climbers that are producing flowers only on their uppermost stems and which are bare at the base can be encouraged into new growth by cutting any weak stems right back to the base and pruning strong shoots hard. Take the opportunity to repaint or repair your support if it needs it at the same time.

> ### Winter protection for roses
>
> Although most roses grown in a temperate climate do not need winter protection, they can die in harsh winters if left exposed. If you live in an area where there are severe winters or bouts of prolonged frost, protect your roses by piling up earth or packing straw (loosely tied in place) around the base of the plant. It may also be worth loosely wrapping the top of the plant in horticultural fleece. Remove protection in spring, before new growth begins.

Generally speaking, you should leave the main stems alone, but if one is exceeding its allotted space then cut it back to size. You can also cut back main shoots if the rose becomes very bare at the base. In that case, cut one or two of them hard back and new growth should come from lower down.

Prune ramblers in summer after flowering, but again, do not prune in the first year. After that, remove two or three entire main stems each year after flowering. It is usually easier to remove them in sections. Cut back each remaining main stem by about one-quarter, and sideshoots by two-thirds. Over-congested plants can become vulnerable to fungal disease.

Reviving a neglected rose

If you inherit an old or neglected climbing rose, you may be able to coax it back to life with hard pruning. Take care with old and fragile specimens as hard pruning can sometimes stop growth completely. To avoid this, rejuvenate climbing roses in stages over two or three years, removing a third of the old stems each year.

In the case of old ramblers, reduce to five or six young and vigorous shoots and reduce side shoots by two thirds. Prune the leading shoots to encourage growth lower down. Feed rejuvenated roses with a rose fertiliser and lay a mulch of compost around the base each spring.

Climbing plants

A fence, wall, shed or garage – or even the front of your house – clothed in plants has a natural charm and provides living colour. There are plenty of vigorous and easy-to-grow climbers that will conceal almost anything. After initial training and tying in, you can leave the plants to do the rest.

There are so many climbers to choose from that you can find a plant to suit your purpose, whether you want to cover your entire house or just soften an unsightly wall or garage with greenery. Some plants, including ivy and Virginia creeper, are self-clinging. This means that they attach themselves to walls with their own suckers so they don't require supports.

Climbing roses and jasmine have a spreading habit, thrusting their stiff shoots between the struts of a trellis, while clematis species wind themselves around thin supports with their leaf stalks. Other climbers, such as wisteria, wind their shoots upwards through vertical supports such as taut wires. Make sure you choose the right type of support for the plant you want to grow – or the right kind of climber if the support is already in position.

Tips for growing on a wall

The ground is usually dry in what is known as the 'rain shadow' at the base of a wall, so plant climbers around 50cm away from the wall, where rainfall will reach their roots. To help the shoots make contact with the base of the support as quickly as possible, settle plants in at an angle, leaning them in towards the wall.

If growing climbers against your house, make sure that no soil piles up above the level of the house's damp-proof course – visible as a line of slate, damp-proof membrane or a wide course of concrete in between rows of bricks.

The soil near walls and fences is often poor, so make the planting hole at least one-and-a-half times as wide and as deep as the rootball and backfill with good garden compost. If planting roses or wisteria,

ensure that the lumpy graft union, visible on the main stem, is at least 2.5cm below the surface. Train the shoots onto your support, fanning them out and securing with twine. Self-clinging climbers don't need support, but hold the shoots in place with sticky tape until they start to cling on their own.

Climbers will not damage a wall whose surface is intact. They can even provide insulation and protection against the weather, with rain sliding off their leaves and away from the wall. But if the façade of a wall or house is damaged in any way do not plant any climbers against it, especially ivy or other self-clinging varieties. Plants with a twining habit or those with aerial roots or tendrils can force their way into cracks or gaps in the masonry, widening them and causing more serious defects.

If you want access to the wall behind a climber attach the base of the trellis to a wall-mounted support with hinges. Attach hooks to the top of the trellis and screw metal eyelets into a corresponding support. Simply unhook to lift the trellis away from the wall.

A plastic-covered metal framework offers ideal support.

Keep an eye on climbers to make sure they don't reach into or along the guttering, window ledges or roofs.

You can also use climbers to cover unattractive features in the garden, such as bins and oil tanks, that cannot be moved out of sight. First you need to create a support; drive posts into the ground around the item you want to conceal and link them with a suitable structure. Trellis is ideal and can be bought ready made in most garden centres and DIY stores. You could also string wire between the posts, using tension screws so that the tension can be regulated. Make sure you leave some access space, as required. Climbing plants can be trained along the

Wall supports for climbing plants

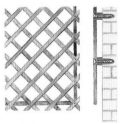

1 Diagonal trellis is ideal for climbing plants that spread out in a fan shape. Garden centres normally stock a wide range of different types and sizes.

2 Lengths of wire, usually plastic covered, attached either vertically or horizontally, make good supports for wisteria-type twining plants.

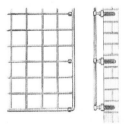

3 Wire or plastic mesh is good for plants that attach themselves with tendrils, allowing the plants ample opportunity to get a good grip.

wires or trellis and should develop quickly to form a dense curtain of foliage and seasonal flowers. Ivy is a perfect plant for the job; fast-growing, vigorous and evergreen, it will offer cover all year round. For abundant flowers, try *Clematis montana*; this climber will be smothered with white or pink blooms in spring, although the leaves fall in autumn.

Trees and shrubs

Give your garden a living framework and ensure year-round colour with some well-chosen trees and shrubs. They can give your garden a sense of maturity too, even when still young, or act as focal points in other planting schemes. Easy to maintain, they make perfect permanent garden features.

Trees and shrubs are the ultimate in long-lasting, low-maintenance garden plants. They can divide a garden into different areas and provide interesting focal points. They offer privacy and natural shade for you as well as shelter and food for birds and other creatures.

Evergreens offer year-round interest and welcome greenery in winter. Deciduous trees mark the seasons as they change; many have beautiful leaf colour as the foliage unfurls in spring or before it falls in autumn. Even in winter, the distinctive silhouettes of bare trees are attractive. In spring and summer, blossom provides interest and colour, while in autumn fruits and berries introduce vibrant new hues.

Long-term garden residents

You may opt for a tree or group of shrubs rather than a flowerbed; you may decide on evergreens rather than deciduous trees and shrubs. Whatever your choice, one thing is certain, your final selection of trees and shrubs will have a long-lasting impact on the development of your garden.

The successful integration of trees and shrubs into the rest of the garden depends upon them being compatible in both size and style. There is a tree for almost any garden, from small to large. When choosing a tree, don't pick something that will outgrow its situation. As a rule, trees in excess of 10m are too large for most gardens and need too much maintenance.

You should be aware of the spread of the roots of trees and shrubs, and plant them at a safe distance from your house and neighbouring properties, so as not to risk damaging the foundations of buildings or underground pipes.

Mark out a new shrubbery bed and then remove any turf or weeds. Dig over and loosen the soil, working in some compost or manure. Hoe the soil to break up the last lumps. The bed can be bordered with edging stones.

You should also consider the spread of a tree's branches as well as its height. Some trees grow as wide as they are tall and their spread may obscure too much of your outlook and create too much shade in a small garden. Trees that have oval, rounded and weeping shapes generally take up more space than those that are columnar, conical or pyramidal.

The shrubbery

To create an interesting and varied bed, combine shrubs of different shapes and varying heights, remembering to plant taller species at the back and lower-growing varieties towards the front.

A mixed group of deciduous and evergreen shrubs involves little work but looks attractive all year round. Its dense growth makes it a good windbreak or a screen for privacy. Once established, shrubs don't require special attention, and the bed will soon develop into a feature that looks as good as a herbaceous border but needs much less care.

Apart from their distinctive shapes, some shrubs have special qualities that enhance the garden through the seasons. Red-barked dogwood or white-stemmed bramble make

Dealing with weeds

Persistent weeds, such as ground elder, couch grass, stinging nettles and brambles, are often widespread under shrubs and trees. They become tangled up in the root systems, making them very difficult to eradicate. They will compete with shrubs and trees for nutrients so must be removed.

One of the best ways to tackle weeds is the most old-fashioned; simply pull them out, preferably on a dry sunny day in spring, when any remains left lying around will wilt quickly. An easier and less time-consuming option is to mulch. Applying a layer of mulch in spring is a good eco-friendly way of tackling weeds; the lack of light and air simply kills them.

■ **Organic mulch** Try a bark mulch or wood chips, which decompose slowly. Spread them in a layer several centimetres thick, making sure the mulch does not touch the trunk or stems. You can mulch with grass cuttings if you are sure they are weed-free, but leave them to wilt first or they will attract snails.

■ **Other materials** Suppress weeds with layers of newspaper, weighed down with soil or grass clippings (top left) or opaque polythene sheeting weighed down with stones (below left); you can also hide these under a layer of bark. You can buy special mulch matting made of hemp or flax, or use a layer of gravel.

■ **Ground-cover** Alternatively, plant shade-loving ground-cover plants. Good choices are purple-leaved varieties of bugle or variegated white dead-nettle. Weeds will no longer thrive once these plants have carpeted the ground beneath shrubs and trees. Only do this around plants that are a few years old.

striking additions to a winter border. *Viburnum* x *bodnantense* produces masses of sweetly fragrant pale pink flowers in winter, all the more surprising and delightful at this bleak time of year.

Spring is heralded with a riot of yellow forsythia; summer sees foliage shrubs come into their own, with many exciting variegated varieties. In autumn the foliage and berries of plants such as cotoneaster and firethorn add brilliant colour that often persists well into winter.

These stars of the shrubbery are at their most spectacular against a backdrop of less showy companions. Good foils include evergreens such as common or cherry laurel, or deciduous forsythia, which – after a burst of yellow blooms in spring – retires greenly into the background.

Care-free plants

To give your trees and shrubs a healthy start, dig over the ground before planting and enrich it with compost or humus. Water regularly for the first few weeks after planting and then during dry spells for the first three years. In early years, keep an area around trees or shrubs free of weeds or other plants. Flowering shrubs need only occasional pruning (see opposite): cut off spring flowers once they are over and prune summer flowering shrubs in late winter or spring. Some varieties thrive on neglect and will flower profusely with no pruning at all.

TIP Choose slow-growing shrubs or trees that do not need much pruning. Japanese maple (*Acer japonicum*), serviceberry (*Amelanchier*) and witch hazel (*Hamamelis*) are all fine examples, as are dogwood (*Cornus*) and viburnums.

Pruning deciduous flowering shrubs helps to keep them tidy and control their spread. It also encourages new flowering shoots to grow and ensures the best display of blossom. This can be done every year but most shrubs can be left quite happily for two or three years between each pruning.

Many flowering shrubs provide colour and fragrance for several weeks. Pruning controls both the growth and flowering potential of your shrubs, as it encourages new shoots. Always angle any cut slightly above an outward facing bud, taking care not to damage the bud, and don't leave any branch stumps projecting.

If you need to remove a branch completely, cut it off cleanly at the base. If you want to shorten it to encourage the shrub to bush out, make a cut immediately above an outward facing bud, which will produce strong growth.

Basic pruning guide

As a rule, evergreen shrubs need little pruning to shape them – all you need do is remove dead, diseased or crossing branches. Deciduous flowering shrubs require a bit more attention and any that are left untended for too long can become straggly.

Prune shrubs that flower on the previous season's growth straight after flowering. Prune those that flower on the new season's growth in spring. Cut back flowering shoots to two or three buds from their junction with the main stem. It's also a good idea to cut some stems down to the base to keep an open framework. Remove any dead, diseased and damaged wood.

Finally, remove any suckers (shoots that rise from the plant below ground level) by tearing them off rather than cutting as this can encourage regrowth. Most shrubs can be left two to three years between pruning; buddleja, however, is so vigorous that it must be pruned hard every year.

TIP Choose the right tool for the job. Sharp secateurs are vital if you want to cut cleanly and avoid crushing any stems. Long-handled loppers will ensure you can prune tall shrubs and extendible loppers enable you to reach even the most distant of branches.

Spring-flowering shrub Summer-flowering shrub

Prune spring-flowering shrubs (left) lightly after flowering, cutting a few stems down to the base. Prune summer-flowering shrubs (right) more vigorously after flowering. Prune both types annually, or every two to three years to keep them tidy and promote flowering.

50 A flowering hedge

The ideal garden boundary, a flowering hedge will enclose your plot with a natural wall of colour and greenery. Once planted, such a hedge can be left to its own devices and will take up a lot less time than more formal clipped structures. Its flowers can be as showy as any herbaceous border.

A flowering shrub like spiraea makes a wonderful hedge and can transform a boundary into a wall of blossom.

A flowering hedge makes a truly easy-care boundary, as you can leave it to grow naturally with little trimming. However, you must make sure that you have enough room for it – you should allow for a width of at least 2m, if not more. Anything less will limit the hedge's potential for producing lots of flowers and this will mean less food and less space for garden wildlife, as well as a less attractive feature.

A hedge can be the ideal boundary structure. It brings colour and interest into the garden and can be as effective and secure as a wall or a fence. Choose thorny plants, such as roses or firethorns, and their prickly branches can form a formidable barrier; it may be possible to climb over a wall or fence but what intruder would attempt to scale a viciously spiny hedge?

Create an informal look by planting a hedge of mixed shrubs, including plants that have different flowering seasons and which produce various colours of foliage and ornamental fruit. This will give your hedge year-round interest. On the other hand, an informal hedge consisting of a single variety of shrub, such *Spiraea* 'Arguta' or *Rosa rugosa*, can be just as attractive.

Plant in autumn

Early autumn is the best time to plant hedging shrubs as it ensures that the root systems have time to establish themselves before the first winter frosts, after which the plants will enter their dormant period. Hedges planted in spring develop quickly above ground, but this leaves their roots unable to keep pace.

Before you begin, mark out the position of your hedge (see below), ensuring that it lies entirely inside your property. Choose bushy plants, one to three years old, and pick species that produce plenty of sideshoots when trimmed. The distance you should leave between each plant varies according to the species or variety; ask the nursery or garden centre for advice.

By and large, deciduous hedging shrubs require little attention after planting, flourish in almost any garden soil and are rarely affected by garden pests. Water a newly planted hedge thoroughly during any dry periods in the first year to prevent damage from drought, and give hedges an annual spring treat of well-rotted compost to encourage growth and bud formation; they should remain healthy for years.

Pruning for hedges

Spring-flowering shrubs, including forsythia, bridal-wreath spiraea, ornamental currant bushes and weigela, begin forming flower buds in the autumn on one or two-year-old growth. To help shrubs retain as many flowering stems as possible, just cut back the oldest and most vigorous new growth every two or three years. Slow-growing shrubs, such as viburnum or flowering dogwood, do best if left unpruned altogether.

Hedges made of summer-flowering species and wild roses need only their dead wood pruned. Although cultivated roses may benefit from deadheading, easy-going wild roses should be left well alone. Their flowers will be replaced by brightly coloured hips that are decorative in their own right – a delight to the gardener for being both low maintenance and visually appealing.

Reviving untidy hedges

Untended hedges of shrubs can become so dense that light is blocked out, so they lose their leaves from the centre outwards and flower only sparsely. To revive them, cut each individual shrub right back to just above ground level – but do this one side at a time so that you still have some hedge during this renewal process.

Planting a hedge

1 Before planting a hedge mark it out with a piece of string. Dig a trench along this line, twice the width of the rootball of the shrubs, but the same depth.

2 Place the shrubs at evenly spaced intervals along the trench, using a tape measure for accuracy. Refill the trench with the excavated soil, firming well around the base of each plant.

3 Prune back any long, non-sprouting branches immediately after planting in order to encourage vigorous new growth. Water in well and cover the ground between the plants with a layer of mulch or bark chippings.

Easy-care containers

Containers of flowering plants are a quick solution for problematic parts in your garden – pop a pot in a bare patch and bring colour to an otherwise awkward spot. They can be used to brighten up courtyards, balconies, decking and patios, too.

Most plants will happily grow in containers as long as they have enough room for their roots. Hardy evergreen trees and shrubs can remain outside in their containers throughout the year. Climbers can be grown in pots and trained to climb up trellis and other supports. For spring colour, plant crocuses and daffodils and other early-flowering plants such as pansies and primroses. Then replant tubs with summer bedding to carry on the show until autumn.

Choose a container the right size for your chosen plant and put a layer of stones or broken crockery in the base for good drainage; then fill it with soil. You can buy specially formulated compost for container plants from garden centres – it's loose, fine and crumbly, and retains water and nutrients but allows excess water to filter through. You can add slow-release fertilisers and water-retaining granules to keep the growing medium moist and fertile.

What to plant

Choose healthy, strongly developed specimens with compact growth and plenty of buds. Combine trailing plants with tall, dense, bushy plants in a single container for visual interest and effect. In terms of colours, you can go for complementary shades or vibrant contrasts. Red, orange and yellow are warm and radiant; blue is fresh and makes a space look larger. Pastels are pretty and white works with all colours. Combinations of yellow and white make dark corners lighter and more welcoming.

If you want long-term pleasure from a pot of flowers, you will have to put in a little work. Regular watering and feeding are essential to stop plants from wilting and to

Ways to cut down on watering

Try these tips to save time on watering:
- Use a planter that has a reservoir of water below a false floor. Wicks steadily draw the water into the compost. An indicator shows the water level so that you can keep the reservoir topped up.
- Put capillary matting in the bottom of a container before planting it up – this retains water which is absorbed as needed by the soil and roots.
- Use special products such as granules, which retain water, or stand containers on water-absorbent matting.
- Insert watering balls – decorative glass balls with long tubes that are filled with water – into the soil; these allow water to seep into the compost gradually and evenly.
- Instal a drip irrigation system – thin pipes with drip heads connected to a hose.

Plants grown in small containers can be blown over in bad weather. Add stability by placing them inside a larger 'cache pot'. Weigh down the larger container with coarse gravel or a few heavy stones filled in with sand. Layer a piece of fleece or a filter mat on top of the stones before positioning the secondary container on top. This helps the plant to take up moisture from the outer pot.

provide the nourishment for abundant flowering. Water containers once a day, in either early morning or late afternoon so the water does not evaporate before it has had a chance to sink in. On very hot days, you may need to water more often. Slow-release fertilisers can be added to the compost in a pot to reduce the number of times you need to feed the plants.

Save time spent tidying up your container plants by choosing species that flower prolifically but which don't need regular deadheading to thrive. Lobelias, *Scaevola* and busy lizzies are ideal. Other species, such as *Diascia* or *Bidens ferulifolia*, like being cut back occasionally. However, verbenas, pelargoniums and osteospermums need regular deadheading.

Growing plants in pots allows you to combine colours in new ways by simply moving containers into new groupings.

If you want an eye-catching feature on your patio or decking, then plant a tub with flowering climbers; you will have both height and colour as they grow upward. All you need is a large container, some potting compost, a sturdy support and a vigorous plant.

Vigorous annual climbers such as black-eyed Susan, nasturtium, sweet pea, morning glory – or even scarlet runner beans – can create a pyramid of flowers quickly and easily. They must be sown or planted afresh every year, but they more than repay the effort with their rapid growth and abundant flowers. As annuals, they do not need overwintering – simply pull out withered stems and start again next spring.

A charming effect can be achieved by planting different annuals in the same container. A mix of morning glory, black-eyed Susan and firecracker vine will produce flowers from early summer right through to autumn. To get the most from these climbing plants, make sure the container you choose is big enough and the compost has good water retention.

A perennial planter

Perennial and shrubby climbers are also suitable for containers and tubs and if they are winter-hardy, they can stay outside all year round. Planting a climbing rose and clematis together produces a spectacular display. The rose climbs up your chosen support, while the clematis winds itself around the rose.

To thrive, these deep rooting plants need a large container – at least 50cm deep – and will need repotting from time to time (roughly every three or four years). Clematis is not particularly demanding but does like to keep its roots cool and shaded; place some pieces of broken ceramic flower pot or tile on the soil around the base of the plant. The late-flowering *Clematis viticella* and *C. integrifolia* are good for containers.

Climbing-plant combinations for pots

Plants	Special features
Clematis viticella 'Huldine' with *Rosa* 'Crimson Shower'	*C. viticella* 'Huldine' bears large white blooms. The rambling rose has crimson double flowers.
Morning glory (*Ipomoea tricolor* 'Heavenly Blue') with a sweet pea (*Lathyrus odoratus* 'Noel Sutton')	The flowers of this morning glory are an intense sky-blue. This blue-flowered sweet pea is highly scented. Deadhead the sweet pea to ensure continuous flowering.
Black-eyed Susan (*Thunbergia alata*) with nasturtium (*Tropaeolum majus*)	Black-eyed Susan has flowers in shades of yellow to orange. Nasturtium's blooms are yellow, orange or red.
Canary creeper (*Tropaeolum peregrinum*) with scarlet runner beans (*Phaseolus coccineus*)	Canary creeper produces masses of yellow flowers in summer and autumn, while the runner beans produce edible beans after their scarlet flowers.
Cup-and-saucer vine (*Cobaea scandens*) with Chilean glory vine (*Eccremocarpus scaber*)	Both species are half-hardy perennials, generally grown as annuals. Both flower through summer to the first frosts, *Cobaea* with violet blooms, *Eccremocarpus* with orange.

Creating a planted pyramid

1 Place stones or a pieces of broken clay pot over the drainage hole and fill the container with potting compost. Add the plant or plants.

2 Push several long, canes or sturdy sticks deep into the soil at regular intervals around the edge of the pot.

3 Tie the sticks firmly together and carefully guide the climbing shoots up them, tying them in with twine as necessary.

Stylish climbing supports

You can buy all sorts of climbing supports, but you can also make your own. Freshly cut willow canes are particularly suitable for shaping into original and attractive climbing supports as they are both strong and pliable.

Perennial climbers such as clematis or rambling roses need sturdy supports. Anchor a wire or wooden trellis firmly in the planter or build a sturdy pyramid. Position the planter in front of a wall or against a fence to stop the support being damaged by strong winds.

By contrast, annual climbers require a great deal less effort and expense. Supports do not have to be so robust for these short-lived plants and you can make them yourself from canes or unusually shaped branches tied together. Create a simple pyramid by using three bamboo canes or hazel sticks tied together at the top. Shoots can be held in place with soft twine, plant ties, or for a novel twist try using wooden clothes pegs – but take care not to squash the soft stems.

Morning glory and nasturtium make a colourful combination.

Colourfully planted hanging baskets can have a dramatic impact. Suspend them from a tree or pergola to draw the eye upwards or hang them by the house and bring the garden closer to home. Choose trailing plants to create a mass of colour that will cover the container beneath.

Hanging baskets festooned with beautiful flowers are a delightful welcoming feature by a front door, as well as enhancing a balcony or patio. Containers are available in terracotta, wicker, plastic and wire. You can mount half-baskets directly to a wall or suspend pots using various kinds of brackets and supports. Choose plants to suit your container, creating an informal jumble of cottagey plants in a rustic wicker basket or a mass of a single pink fuchsia in galvanised metal.

Plant the whole basket

A liner is essential to retain the soil in a basket and there are many different kinds available, including hessian and moss and some, such as those made of coconut fibre, with holes pre-punched for planting. When a basket is suspended above eye level, the lining looks pretty ugly. Hide it by planting through the sides as well as in the top of the basket. Insert plants through the holes: trailing plants like lobelia and petunia work as well planted in the sides of hanging baskets as in the top.

Don't forget to water

The soil dries out particularly quickly in hanging baskets because there is no rigid container to retain moisture, but you can buy containers with a water reservoir in the base, which allows water to be taken up gradually by the absorbent liner. When watering, it's a good idea to fit an extension attachment (a long pipe with a fine spout or rose that turns down at the end) to your watering can or hose pipe so you can water hanging containers without using a ladder or taking them down. Alternatively, choose a bracket that incorporates a pulley, allowing you to lower the basket easily for watering.

Planting a hanging basket

1 If your hanging basket has a rounded base place, it in a large bucket whilst planting to keep it stable. Putting a few large stones and/or some water in the bucket beforehand will make it even more stable.

2 Now fill the container about two-thirds full with fresh potting compost. Add a slow-release fertiliser to the soil at this stage, following the instructions on the pack. This will keep the plants well nourished for weeks. You can also add water-retaining granules to the compost.

3 Insert the plants in the compost, planting them at the same depth as they were in their propagating pots. Fill in the gaps with compost and firm everything in place. Now water the newly planted container thoroughly and hang it in position.

Container maintenance

To get the most out of your containers, they will need some occasional care. This may be repotting over-grown containers or providing some form of protection during the harsher days of winter. Follow these simple guidelines and your potted plants should flourish.

When you water a container-grown shrub or small tree, does the water run straight out through the bottom of the container? If so, the compost is depleted and the plant needs repotting. If you don't wish to repot immediately, you can buy some time by top dressing. Loosen and remove the top 5–10cm of soil. Replace it with fresh compost, ideally adding a slow-release fertiliser at the same time, and repot as soon as convenient.

Most plants need repotting after two or three years. If you need to move the old container before repotting, do this while the compost is dry and move large pots on a plant dolly. Water the plant thoroughly and leave for a couple of hours before carefully removing it. With large, heavy plants, lay the pot on its side, loosen the soil all around and pull the root ball out. Remove as much of the old compost as possible from the root ball, as well as damaged roots. If it is compacted, loosen the edges of the root ball with a hand fork to encourage new growth. The new container should be roughly 2–4cm larger in diameter than the old one.

Drainage layer

Put a layer of broken ceramic pots (also known as crocks) and some stones in the base of the new pot to facilitate drainage. Then add fresh compost until the pot is about two-thirds full. Set the plants in the pot and fill in with more compost. Make sure

Make the job of moving heavy containers easier by using a plant dolly; ease the pot onto the dolly and then simply push to its new position.

Plants for pots that overwinter outside

Plant	Winter location/advice
Grasses, such as maiden grass (*Miscanthus sinensis*)	Position the pot in a spot that is not too damp, if possible.
Evergreens, such as box (*Buxus*) and rhododendron	Protect from bright sunlight. Wrap the containter to protect the roots and water occasionally.
Conifers	Place in a shady spot. Wrap the pot warmly; water occasionally.
Deciduous native trees and shrubs	If possible, do not allow to become too damp. Wrap pot well.
Herbaceous perennials such as phlox, delphinium and *Coreopsis*	Ideally, place pots under an overhanging roof. Ensure there is a sufficient drainage layer in the pot.

the plant is standing straight and is at the same depth as before. The top of the soil should be at least 2cm below the rim so you can water without compost spilling out over the top. Firm in and water well; if the level of compost then sinks, add some more.

Winter protection

Many container plants come from warmer climes and cannot survive winter outdoors. This means that plants like bougainvillea, brugmansia or Chinese lantern must be moved indoors before the first frosts; a temperate greenhouse or cool conservatory, at about 7°C, should be fine. Other plants, such as olives, oleander and bay trees will survive some frost and need only be moved in when the temperature is below freezing for long periods.

Frost-resistant plants, such as small conifers or deciduous trees, roses, rhododendron and box, can winter outside, provided their roots are kept warm and they are sheltered from the wind. The greatest threat to bulbs and hardy deciduous shrubs comes from prolonged wet weather, so these should be sheltered from the rain.

The soil in a pot freezes faster than that in a border or bed and then the roots cannot draw up any moisture. To prevent this, wrap the containers in an insulating material such as hessian or bubble wrap packed with straw; secure by tying in place with garden twine.

Wrap the plants in hessian, horticultural fleece or rush matting – but not bubble wrap as it doesn't 'breathe'. Gather together the leaves of palms and cordyline, tying them together to protect their crowns. Wrap the trunks and crowns of tree ferns with fleece or hessian stuffed with straw.

Even in winter, evergreens such as dwarf pines, box or rhododendron lose water through their leaves, especially on mild, sunny days. Move them to a shady spot and water now and again on frost-free days.

In winter, protect the tender tips of any plant that is not fully hardy by covering loosely with horticultural fleece, hessian or an old blanket; tie it with twine. If further protection is needed, wrap the plant and pot in hessian or bubble wrap and stuff with straw.

A paved area can be the perfect spot in your garden to set aside for seating. It makes a charming setting for containers and tubs and you can plant up any gaps or cracks between the stones with flowering plants, surrounding yourself with colour and scent.

A patio is the perfect place to relax and unwind. You can arrange a table and chairs on the paving and enjoy mealtimes outdoors or add a bench to create a quiet corner from which to contemplate the garden. Once laid, a paved area is fairly easy to maintain; just wash it down occasionally and weed between the cracks.

You can introduce plants to a paved area with containers and tubs, and by changing them as the season progresses, you ensure year-round colour. It is also possible to incorporate planting in the paving itself, in gaps between slabs. There may also be enough space around the edges of a paved area to plant perennials. Scented plants are ideal; pick night-scented flowers such as *Nicotiana* or stocks, especially if you plan to sit outdoors in the evenings.

If your patio is not sheltered or shaded by a building or wall then you can surround it with a trellis or pergola and cover this with a vigorous climbing plant. Alternatively, position tall-growing shrubs around the edges of the paving. If the patio is very

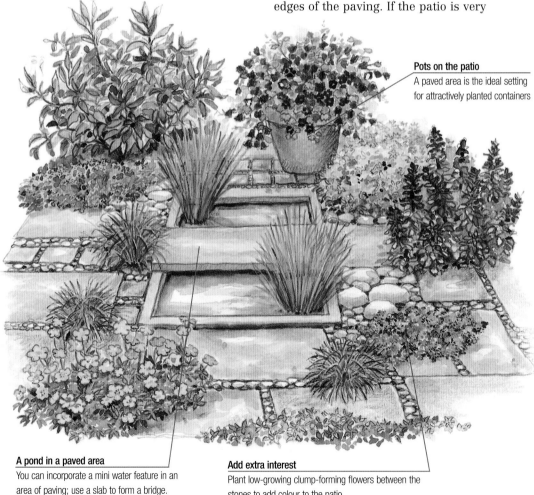

Pots on the patio
A paved area is the ideal setting for attractively planted containers

A pond in a paved area
You can incorporate a mini water feature in an area of paving; use a slab to form a bridge.

Add extra interest
Plant low-growing clump-forming flowers between the stones to add colour to the patio.

Plants for paved areas

Plant	Botanical name
Biting stonecrop	*Sedum acre*
Rock rose	*Helianthemum nummularium*
New Zealand bur	*Acaena* species
Saxifrage	*Saxifraga* species
Corsican mint	*Mentha requienii*
Bugle	*Ajuga reptans*
Pearlwort	*Sagina subulata*
Thyme	*Thymus* species
Toadflax	*Linaria* species
Variegated ground ivy	*Glechoma hederacea* 'Variegata'
Spring gentian	*Gentiana verna*
Chamomile	*Chamaemelum nobile*

exposed during the hottest part of the day then you could use an awning or parasol for easy and effective shade.

Planting in paving

Gaps between paving slabs and large cracks in the stones can be filled with plants. First remove weeds from the cracks and gaps. Then fill them with sand, fine chippings or gravel, brushing it in with a broom, and lightly hose over the area. Using a finger or a dibber to make holes, insert your chosen plants. Low-maintenance, clump-forming species are best, especially those that don't mind being trodden on. Good choices include self-seeding species, such as dwarf snapdragons, and scented plants like thyme and chamomile.

In larger areas of paving, soften the expanse of stone by lifting the occasional slab and filling the holes with plants. Dig over the soil beneath and add a mixture of sand and fine gravel. Now you can plant up with carpet-forming varieties, cushion-style rock garden plants or low-growing grasses or shrubs. Before long your old patio will have a charming rustic look that requires minimal maintenance.

A paved area under trees provides shade and seclusion.

62 Patio water garden

Building a pond can be big job but you can easily construct a less time-consuming water feature from an old half beer barrel. These wooden containers need only be made watertight to be transformed into a small, low-maintenance water garden.

Many garden centres stock wooden half beer barrels, which make ideal tubs for patio water gardens as they are frost-resistant and relatively portable. The barrel must be watertight and clean inside before it can be used. Clean it thoroughly with environmentally friendly detergent and plenty of water. Then line with heavy-duty plastic pond liner: you must line any tub treated with tar as this will kill water plants. Smooth the liner against the tub walls and pour in a layer of gravel and soil – either a loamy garden soil or special pond compost. (Don't use normal garden compost in a water garden – it contains too many nutrients and will trigger an explosion of

Creating a pond need not be a chore; you can turn something as simple as a half beer barrel into a stunning water feature.

Water plants for tubs

Ideal bog plants (top left) for a tub are marsh marigold (*Caltha palustris*), pennywort (*Hydrocotyle vulgaris*), candelabra primula and water avens. Plant them in pots 50–60cm in diameter, in moist, loamy soil, and in water 5cm deep.

Ideal shallow marginals (left) are sedge (*Carex*), bog arum (*Calla palustris*), buckbean (*Menyanthes trifoliata*) and arrowhead (*Sagittaria*). Plant them in pots 50–60cm in diameter, in loam or pond compost, and in water 8–10cm deep. Keep a third of the water surface plant free.

Ideal deep marginals (bottom left) are sweet sedge (*Acorus calamus*), flowering rush (*Butomus umbellatus*) and sweet galingale (*Cyperus longus*). Plant them in pots 50–100cm in diameter, in loam or pond compost, and in water 15–30cm deep. Cover the soil with pebbles to keep it in place.

algae.) Then top up with water so that the liner is flattened against the sides. Tack the liner around the rim, above the water line, and trim off any excess.

The right plants

If you want to grow bog and moisture-loving plants, your tub will need deep, very moist soil, as found at the edge of a wild pond. Once planted and soaked with water, mulch with organic matter to keep the moisture in. To grow shallow marginal plants, you need to replicate a pond margin, where plants grow with their roots in soil in shallow water, around 8–10cm in depth. Deeper marginals will grow in a larger tub and need 15–30cm depth of water. Some aquatics need deeper water than this to thrive and will not be suitable for a tub water garden.

Small ponds heat up quickly and should not be exposed to direct sunlight for more than six hours a day. Try, therefore, to position your patio water garden in a quiet corner that only gets sun in the late afternoon and evening. If your patio is too sunny, place a bushy plant in an adjacent container to provide some shade over the water-filled tub. You could even put up a parasol at midday. Whatever shade you provide, it's important to check the water level and top it up occasionally with water from a butt – never straight from the tap.

Planting and maintenance

Plant aquatics between late spring and mid summer, when they are in active growth, the water is warm and light levels are good. Don't buy too many plants – three or four are enough for a container 50–60cm in diameter. A single species can be just as decorative as a mixed planting.

A half beer barrel is frost-resistant so will not need cleaning out before winter or protection during cold spells. Remove dead plant parts by cutting them off carefully below the water surface. If plants grow too quickly, remove part of them in late spring after the dormant winter period.

Pond care

A garden pond closely modelled on nature provides an attractive habitat for plant and animal wildlife. But even the most natural pond will benefit from some basic maintenance. Look after your aquatic plants and keep the water clear to avoid time-consuming jobs later.

You may have had the good fortune to have inherited a pond when you moved into your house. If you want to keep it looking good and preserve a healthy habitat for wildlife and plants, you will have to follow a few simple maintenance guidelines. Neglect a pond and it will soon become overgrown and choked with pondweed, a place where no aquatic plants or animals could flourish.

Spring and summer care

Towards the end of spring cut off any dead plant material poking above the surface of the water and put it on the compost heap. From May onwards, when the water has warmed up slightly, divide and replant any bog plants and water lilies that have grown too large. Take great care when doing this, as many frogs and toads will have spawned in March and it is important not to disturb their eggs.

By early summer, algae have often colonised the water surface, which is now heating up rapidly. A sudden explosion of algae growth, known as an algal bloom, can turn the water's surface completely green, almost like a lawn. Aquatic plants in the deeper, cooler water may have trouble competing with algae for space and nutrients. If you are patient, you will find that microorganisms will eat up the algae in just a few days and the water will clear.

Bog and water plants, which take up a lot of nutrients during the summer, may help to prevent an algal bloom occurring later on in

A piece of netting stretched across a pond will catch autumn leaves. Use tall wooden posts as supports if you want to raise the netting above the level of marginal plants to avoid squashing their upper leaves.

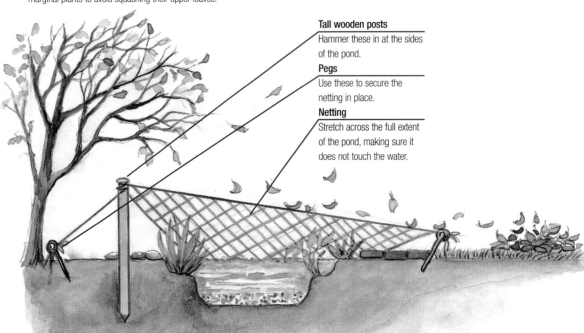

Tall wooden posts
Hammer these in at the sides of the pond.

Pegs
Use these to secure the netting in place.

Netting
Stretch across the full extent of the pond, making sure it does not touch the water.

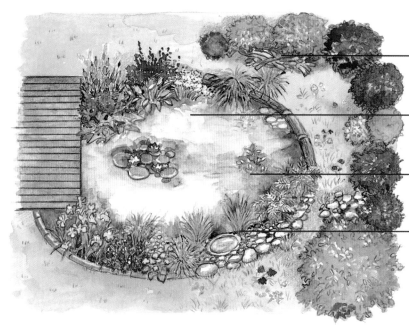

Dead wood
Winter accommodation for toads, frogs and newts.

Clean water
Water needs to be clean for fish to thrive.

Water margins
An important habitat for plants and animals.

Sloping sides
A slope at one edge of the pond makes it easier for certain animals to crawl in and out of the water.

A pond can be home to a myriad of creatures; you can preserve their habitat if you just maintain the right conditions.

the year, provided that nutrient levels in the pond are not too high. An occasional algal bloom is natural and no cause for concern, so don't disturb the pond's ecological balance by removing it. If you use an air pump to aerate your pond, start cleaning the filter more regularly.

Don't start feeding fish until the water reaches 10°C, or warmer; if aquatic plants are healthy and growing well, there is no need to give goldfish extra food. Overfeeding will encourage fish to breed more which, in turn, can affect the water quality.

Autumn and winter care

It's best not to site a pond where a lot of leaves can fall into it. If this is unavoidable, stretch some netting over the pond in autumn (see diagram left) to catch fallen leaves, otherwise they sink to the bottom and, together with dead plant material from bog and water plants, form a layer of mulch. Drawing on the oxygen in the water, microorganisms feed on the decaying plants and convert them into mud. This natural process eventually causes a pond to silt up,

and after a few years you will have to clean it out. The fewer leaves that land in your pond in the first place, the longer you will be able to put off this job.

Before the first winter frosts, remove any electrical equipment, such as pumps and lights, from the water. Once winter arrives, do not disturb the pond water or hack at the ice if the pond freezes over – the shock will disturb any hibernating wildlife.

If you want to keep part of the water free of ice, install a floating pool heater, or simply float a tennis ball in the pond. This will keep the water from freezing over completely and allow gases to escape. Aquatic plants also help to prevent the pond from freezing up and provide a habitat for overwintering wildlife at the bottom of the pond.

TIP You can help to prevent the build up of algae over time by avoiding high levels of nutrients in the water. Underwater plants such as curled pondweed (*Potamogeton crispus*) and water violet (*Hottonia palustris*) preserve the natural balance of your pond by taking up large amounts of nutrients from the water. At the same time, they produce plenty of oxygen.

66 Laying a lawn

A lawn gives even the smallest garden a spacious feel. Whether you want a lush formal lawn or simply an area of grass as a play area, it is worth putting in the extra work at the beginning to create a lawn that will be easy to care for and will look good for years to come.

You may want to create a new lawn in your garden or replace an area of worn-out grass. Before you begin laying a lawn, think about how you will be using it. A formal, ornamental lawn looks lovely but isn't much good for family games and parties. For this type of wear, you need to grow a robust grass.

A lawn laid in a simple geometric shape such as a square, rectangle or circle, makes the upkeep much easier. The minimum width for strips of lawn, such as paths between flowerbeds, should be the width of your lawnmower.

You can buy special lawn seed mixtures for almost every purpose. For a fine-bladed, elegant lawn that will receive only little wear, choose common bentgrass (*Agrostis capillaris*) or red fescue (*Festuca rubra*). Extremely resilient grasses, such as smooth-stalked meadow grass (*Poa pratensis*), perennial rye grass (*Lolium perenne*), crested dogtail (*Cynosurus cristatus*) and timothy (*Phleum pratensis* ssp. *bertolinii*) should be chosen for a more hard-wearing lawn, suitable for sports and games.

Good preparation pays off

A robust, low-maintenance, hardwearing lawn will thrive on most normal soils, but the secret to good-looking grass is to prepare the ground properly. Taking time to do jobs that initially seem onerous will save trouble in future years.

The first job is to loosen the soil, and the easiest way to do this is with a rotavator. Hire a petrol-driven machine or use a manual one. Alternatively, dig the ground over with a spade, making sure you work over the soil thoroughly. The top layer of soil should be fine and crumbly, yet firm. Water

Using turf

Rolls of turf allow you to create a neat, green lawn from a bare patch of earth in next to no time. Simply prepare the soil as for sowing a lawn (see right) and roll out the turf sections one by one, laying them flush with one another and tamping them down with the back of a rake. Water regularly until well established.

must be able to seep through the soil properly and air must be able to penetrate deeply enough. Work sand into compact and heavy soils to loosen them. Enrich sparse or light soils with compost.

A bumpy lawn will make mowing more difficult, so level out mounds and hollows, smoothing over the soil with a rake. Remove stones, roots and weeds from the soil – it will pay off later – and let the soil rest for a month. Then rake out any weeds that have sprung up in the meantime.

Lawns need nutrients for healthy growth. Apply a specially formulated lawn fertiliser to the prepared ground, and then set to work sowing lawn seed or laying turf. If sowing seed, do this in spring when the ground is still moist from the previous autumn and winter rains.

Sowing a lawn

1 Before you sow lawn seed, make sure the soil has been properly prepared. Take the time to work it thoroughly with a rotavator or spade.

2 Next, level it off as finely as possible with a rake, removing larger clods, stones and root remains. Then tamp down the surface carefully using the back of the rake.

3 Using a seed spreader and keeping to the recommended quantity, distribute the lawn seed evenly, first lengthways, then crossways over the soil. Rake over the surface lightly.

4 Tamp the seed down with boards or a roller so it makes good contact with the soil, and water well. Protect it from birds if necessary with netting. The seed should germinate within two weeks.

For a beautifully manicured, formal lawn that's easy to look after, lay the grass with neat straight edges.

68 Mowing

Cutting grass encourages it to grow, so regular mowing will ensure the spread of a lush green swathe. By using the right equipment and by following a few basic rules, cutting the grass need not be too time-consuming and your lawn will remain well tended and healthy.

Mowing is essential to achieve a dense, healthy and even lawn. There are a few tips that will help make the job as quick and simple as possible. It's important not to mow the grass if it's wet; it will form clumps and stick to the blades of the mower, clogging it up. Cut the grass regularly so that it doesn't get longer than 8cm high – lawnmowers don't cut long grass effectively. Set the cutting height to maximum for the first cut of the year, then lower it and mow again. In spring and summer, mow an informal lawn once a week. In autumn, once

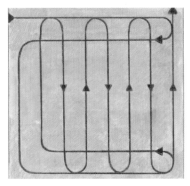

Begin mowing a strip at each end of the lawn, then mow up and down between these two strips, from one side to the other, in rows that slightly overlap.

a fortnight should be fine. Never mow too short or you will expose the grass roots, which may then die and leave bald patches. The ideal length of grass for an informal lawn is 2.5–3.5cm, but let it grow a bit longer in a drought. Use a basket or box attached to your mower to collect the clippings and add these in thin layers to the compost heap.

It is vital to keep the blades of your mower sharp; blunt blades rip instead of cutting and can tear up the roots of the grass. The time of mowing is also important. Mow in the morning or afternoon, when the air is a little cooler. Mowing in the midday sun is hard on both you and your lawn.

What type of mower?

Cylinder mowers produce an extremely fine cut, and are ideal for formal, ornamental lawns. Rotary mowers cut with a horizontally rotating blade, fraying the cut grass slightly in the process. These work well on hardwearing lawns. Choose one with a cutting width of 40–50cm. Another option is an electric hover mower. These are smooth-running and easy to handle. If you have an enormous lawn, you may want to invest in a ride-on lawnmower. You can even buy robot mowers, which mow the lawn for you.

Even the finest lawn with the best-maintained grass will look unkempt if its edges become straggly and the grass spreads unchecked into borders and onto paths. It is difficult to get neat edges with most mowers but there are a range of specialist tools that will make the job quick and easy.

When you trim the edges of your lawn you could use ordinary garden shears, but long-handled edging shears make life a lot easier. The job is even quicker if you have a rolling lawn edger, which cuts with a rotating circular blade (a bit like a pizza cutter), or battery-operated grass shears. A strimmer is useful for edges, slopes and other hard-to-reach places; it cuts the grass with a rotating nylon cord and is powered by electricity, petrol or a rechargeable battery.

As well as regular trimming, you will need to cut the lawn edges neatly twice a year. Use a spade or, better still, a half-moon lawn-edger to cut through the turf into the soil beneath.

Fixed lawn edging

If you want to avoid having to trim and cut edges altogether, you can install fixed edging or lay a strip of bricks or stone blocks around the lawn perimeter. These allow you to mow right up to and over the edges of the grass without affecting the borders.

There are many different types of edging, but whatever you choose it should be laid at ground level, flush with the lawn. One clever solution, available from garden centres and DIY stores, is also easy-to-install. Moulded

Long-handled edging shears or a strimmer (right) will make short work of edging.

Moulded 'L' shaped edging blocks make mowing easier.

'L' shaped edging blocks have a flat section that lies flush with the grass and along which the lawnmower wheels can run. You fit them by digging a shallow trench along the edge of the lawn and laying a bed of sand in the trench; the edging blocks are then laid on top of the sand.

Raised edging made from log rolls, concrete shapes, bricks or tiles don't help much when it comes to cutting lawn edges, as the mower cannot cut right up to them – you will need to use a strimmer or an edger.

If your lawn is growing unevenly or looks pale or yellowish in colour, it may be suffering from a lack of water and nutrients. Prolonged drought will cause withered grass and brown patches, while nutrient deficiencies will result in poor colour and growth.

The threat of drought is a good reason for not laying or seeding a new lawn in summer, especially if hosepipe bans are a regular summer occurrence in your area. Newly laid or seeded lawn must be watered regularly in summer, though an established lawn can survive most ordinary summer droughts. If you can't water, then the best thing you can do for your lawn is to avoid mowing it altogether for a while. During a drought the lawn may look dead, but it will quickly recover when it rains again.

Don't be tempted to water little and often; instead water less frequently but thoroughly. Only water in the early morning or in the evening, so that the water does not evaporate but soaks into the ground.

Lawns often suffer from a lack of nutrients because the grass is constantly drawing nutrients from the soil and then losing them every time it is mowed. Nitrogen deficiency, in particular, is easy to identify – it slows the growth of the grass and causes it to fade to a light green or yellowish colour.

A balanced diet

A specially formulated lawn fertiliser contains all the necessary nutrients – including important trace elements – in a balanced mixture. Give the lawn a good feed at the beginning of the growth period in spring. If you use a slow-release fertiliser, this will save time over the growing season: it releases nutrients gradually, and you only need to apply it once or twice a year.

Never exceed the quantities stated on the packet. Too much fertiliser burns the grass and causes bald patches on the lawn. Spread the fertiliser evenly – an uneven application results in patchy growth and colour. Water generously after applying fertiliser, to wash the nutrients into the soil.

An automatic sprinkler does the watering for you while a lawn-feed spreader (right) makes light work of an important task.

Over time moss and weeds invade most lawns. You can prevent this, and reduce the amount of time spent weeding, by keeping the lawn aerated and by removing any layers of thatch that build up on its surface. A healthy lawn will grow well and hold its own against invasive weeds.

A few daisies in a lawn can look pretty, but grass choked with plantain and dandelions is less attractive. You can remove weeds with a hand fork or a 'daisy grubber', but it is backbreaking work. It is better to keep weeding to a minimum by taking a few preventive measures.

Weeds grow best in neglected lawns, in undernourished grass, although if you provide great growing conditions, both grasses and weeds will shoot up and can be cut with the mower. As weeds are far less tolerant of regular cutting than grass, they will diminish drastically.

Aerating the lawn

When soil in a well-used lawn gets compacted, it is difficult for air and water to reach the roots and the grass grows poorly. To remedy this, first remove the 'thatch' of dead matter that accumulates on the surface of every lawn by raking briskly with a spring-tined rake or a powered lawn rake.

Then aerate the lawn by punching vertical holes into the soil so that air can penetrate. The simplest way to do this is with a garden

A daisy-grubber gets right down to the roots of weeds. Lawn sand (right) spread on an aerated lawn aids drainage.

fork or a hollow-tined aerator. If possible, tackle this job every year or two. Choose damp conditions in spring or autumn, to allow the grass to recover more quickly from the stress.

Afterwards, on a dry day, apply lawn sand at a rate of about half a bucket per square metre, which will improve drainage and help to break up the soil. If your lawn is small, just shovel some sand over it and spread it out with a broom; for larger lawns, use a spreader.

Repairing bad patches

1 Long-lasting repairs for very mossy or damaged lawns are best dealt with by re-sowing. Thoroughly rake the patch to remove moss, the remains of any grass and creeping weeds. Pull up individual deep-rooted weeds by hand.

2 Scatter a fine layer of compost and spread a lawn seed mixture evenly over the prepared ground. Press down firmly with a board – this will prevent the seeds washing away – then water with the hose nozzle set to a fine spray.

72 Ground-cover plants

Plants that spread quickly and cover a lot of ground are ideal for the easy-care garden. They provide a mass of colour, suppress weeds and many grow where grass fails to thrive. Site ground-cover plants beneath trees and on slopes and banks, where they can be left to their own devices.

Ground-cover plants spread to form a dense living blanket in a relatively short space of time. They look attractive and suppress the growth of weeds, making them ideal for a low-maintenance garden. In autumn, ground-cover plants can conceal fallen leaves from deciduous trees and shrubs beneath their own foliage. The fallen leaves then act as a natural compost and insulating blanket. As well as saving you

Golden daffodils break through a carpet of *Pachysandra terminalis*; an evergreen plant with creamy white flowers.

You can encourage ground-cover plants to spread even further. Spread their shoots out over the ground and secure them with pieces of wire bent into a 'U', pressed into the soil over the shoots.

the time that it takes to rake them up, the autumn leaves also make the spreading of fertiliser unnecessary.

Botanically, ground-cover plants are varied. Some are annuals and others are herbaceous perennials or creeping shrubs. What they have in common is the ability to form dense cover in a short space of time by sending out runners or long shoots.

Keep the ground under trees weed-free with shade-loving plants such as cranesbills or bugle. On steep banks at risk of erosion, the roots of ground-cover plants such as *Cotoneaster horizontalis* or *Juniperus horizontalis* will help to prevent soil from being washed away. The low-growing shrubby honeysuckle *Lonicera pileata* or the shade-tolerant *Pachysandra terminalis*, with its deep-green leaves, are also suitable.

Be cautious with vigorous sprawling plants such as periwinkle. Only plant prolific species like these where you can allow them to spread unchecked – otherwise you will need to continually cut them back to keep them under control.

Suitable soil

Once it has become established, a border planted with bushy ground-cover plants needs very little attention. But before it reaches this stage, it is worth taking the trouble to prepare the soil carefully.

Stubborn weeds such as ground elder or couch grass can quickly choke young ground-cover plants, so dig over the earth deep down and clear it of all weeds and root remains. This will spare you some time-consuming weeding while the ground-cover plants get established.

In addition, it is worth improving the soil before you begin planting to give ground-cover plants a good start. Work in compost thoroughly, or mix in blood, fish and bone or some other organic slow-release fertiliser.

Planting ground cover

How far apart you position the plants depends on how prolifically each will grow, as well as on your patience and the amount of money you are prepared to spend. The closer together you plant them, the more quickly you will have dense cover; the greater the distance between plants, the cheaper the outlay. If planting under trees or shrubs, do this in autumn after leaf fall.

For each plant, dig a hole about twice the size of the root ball. Put the plant in, keeping it at the same depth as it was in its original container. Fill in earth all around the plant and firm in. Water thoroughly and ensure that the new plants continue to receive sufficient water, especially as they become established. Prune back ground-cover plants in spring, if you need to keep them in check.

Easy-care kitchen garden

It's simple to create a small area for growing vegetables in most gardens. A vegetable plot need not be hard work if you prepare the ground well and plant just a few favourite varieties. Pick a spot near the house so that the delicious home-grown produce is nearer to the kitchen – and the pot.

A neat, well-tended kitchen garden is a joy to behold and you can combine flowering plants and vegetables for an attractive display.

Choose a sunny, open site for your kitchen-garden plot. Salad plants, cucumbers, peas and beans require plenty of sunshine, and root vegetables, such as carrots and potatoes, will produce a good crop only when their foliage receives sufficient sunlight. Wind can impair growth – a windbreak such as that offered by a low hedge can provide much-needed shelter on a blustery site.

Preparing the patch

On average, a plot of about three square metres should be enough to provide vegetables for a family of four. Start preparing the soil the previous autumn, adding compost to enrich sandy soils, and lightening heavy clays with sand or grit along with your compost. If the soil is very compacted, dig it over in autumn and leave it for the winter to let frost break up the clods. In spring, before sowing or planting, lightly fork over and rake level.

Rotate your crops

Annual vegetables should be rotated from bed to bed each year, completing a 'circuit' in three or four years. This is partly because different crops have different nutrient requirements, but also because growing one type of crop repeatedly in the same bed allows pests and diseases specific to that crop to proliferate. Keep a garden diary to record your system of rotation.

Follow recommended planting distances; plants don't like to be too close together and diseases thrive in cramped conditions. Where possible, choose disease-resistant varieties as these are immune to common problems and often produce higher yields.

Herbs smell delicious, enhance your cooking and provide a haven for butterflies and bees. Many look beautiful too and you can add them to your ornamental beds and borders as well as creating a dedicated herb garden. Best of all, most herbs are quite happy with minimal care.

Herbs are an easy-care garden favourite. Even on poor soil, with just a little attention many species will thrive. Thyme, sage and rosemary release their aroma best in a dry spot in full sun, on poor, well-drained soil. Lovage, chives, parsley and mint grow best in partial sun and in slightly damper humus-rich soils.

A herb garden does not have to be large – just one square metre will support a host of aromatic plants. You need to be able to reach all your herbs easily, so position a few paving stones in the bed. This will provide access and improve the microclimate: the stones will store heat from the sun, releasing it again at night and warming the soil.

Herb cultivation

Sow hardy annual and biennial herbs, such as dill and coriander, straight into the bed from March onwards, making subsequent sowings through summer for a continuous supply of young leaves. Start off heat lovers like basil indoors, or wait until the end of May before sowing outdoors. Sow or plant out perennial herbs such as chives, mint and lemon balm in their growing positions from March onwards. It is a good idea to plant invasive herbs such as mint and tarragon in containers to restrict their spread.

Lightly clip herbs regularly to ensure a permanent supply of fresh young leaves and shoots. Cut back shrubby herbs, such as sage and lavender, by about a third after they have finished flowering. In winter, a mulch will help to protect perennial herbs like rosemary, oregano and sage.

An early start

Buy container-grown herbs that just need planting out – especially varieties such as parsley that are slow and difficult to germinate. This will give you a 3–4 week head start compared with growing herbs from seed.

Rows of aromatic herbs can delight the senses with their scented foliage and delicate flowers.

Raised vegetable beds

If you have only a small space, try growing your vegetables in a raised bed. Since you are filling up the bed with soil and other organic material, there is no digging involved. And the height of the bed saves your back as you won't have to bend so far to tend or pick the crops.

The soil in a raised bed warms up quickly in spring because the sides catch the sun as well as the soil surface. This means you can often sow or plant up a raised bed as much as two weeks earlier than an ordinary vegetable patch.

Ideally, you need more than one raised bed in order to rotate the crops you grow. If you have only one bed then make sure you plant mainly vegetables that are heavy feeders in the first year, when nitrogen levels in the soil are at their highest. As soil nutrients are depleted, plant crops with lower nutrient requirements each year (see below). After about six years, remove the filling of your bed and replace with new layers of organic matter and soil (see right).

Use a raised-bed kit

You can buy wooden or moulded-plastic kits for raised beds, which are quick and easy to erect. The plastic ones simply lock together at the corners and will not rot. Their hollow construction makes them a good insulator, keeping the soil warm and encouraging your crops to grow quickly and strongly.

Making best use of nutrients in a raised bed

Year	Conditions	Planting
1	The bed has a high nitrogen content.	Plants with high nutrient requirements such as sweet peppers, tomatoes and leeks.
2	There is still plenty of nitrogen.	Plants with high nutrient requirements such as cucumbers, courgettes and fennel.
3	Nitrogen content is beginning to decline.	Plants with medium nutrient requirements such as kohlrabi, onions and parsnips.
4	Even less nitrogen available.	Plants with medium to low nutrient needs such as mangetout, radishes and lettuce.
5	The soil now has a comparatively low nitrogen content.	Plants with low nutrient requirements, such as carrots and turnips.
6	The raised bed rots down and nutrients are exhausted.	Plants with low nutrient requirements and nitrogen-fixing plants such as beans, peas, broad beans and potatoes.
7	Refill the raised bed with new soil: conditions are as year 1.	Plants with high nutrient requirements as in the first year.

Making a raised bed

The best time to build a raised bed is autumn, when there is a plentiful supply of organic matter in the garden that you can use for the various layers.The soil in the bed will have enough time to settle and compact over winter.

To make a raised bed from scratch, you will need some fine-mesh wire netting to line the base (to keep out rodents), pond liner (to help retain moisture), thick planks of wood for the sides and sturdy posts for the corners. An area measuring about 1.5m by up to 4m is a good size and the finished bed should reach a working height of 75–90cm.

Dig out the soil to a depth of 25cm and put it to one side. Erect the posts and retaining walls and line the walls with pond liner. Cover the base with the wire netting and add with a layer of twigs and branches. Then add a layer of lightly moistened shredded paper and coarsely chopped garden waste, then a layer of fresh garden waste and autumn leaves. Top off with a layer of compost mixed with the excavated soil.

Every year, top up the bed with compost and fresh soil. Dig it over lightly in spring and cover it with a layer of mulch in autumn. After about six years the soil will be exhausted and you should replace it.

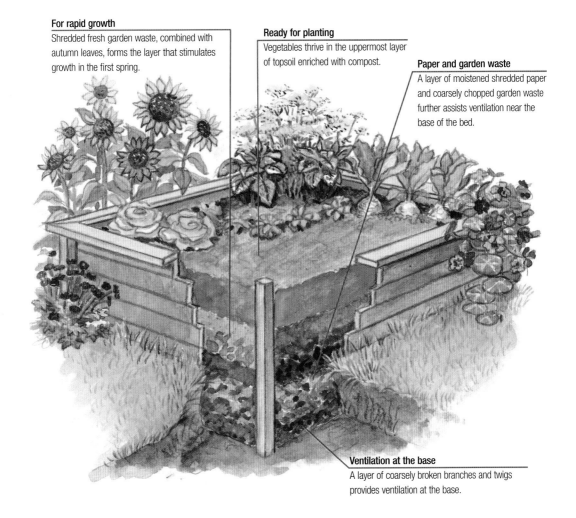

For rapid growth
Shredded fresh garden waste, combined with autumn leaves, forms the layer that stimulates growth in the first spring.

Ready for planting
Vegetables thrive in the uppermost layer of topsoil enriched with compost.

Paper and garden waste
A layer of moistened shredded paper and coarsely chopped garden waste further assists ventilation near the base of the bed.

Ventilation at the base
A layer of coarsely broken branches and twigs provides ventilation at the base.

Pot-grown vegetables

You can grow all sorts of herbs and vegetables in troughs and in containers on a balcony, roof garden or patio. Larger pots will work best as they can hold a greater volume of compost. Choose an attractive container and you can even turn your vegetables and herbs into ornamental features.

Most culinary herbs can be grown in pots: dill, parsley, chives, rosemary and thyme all do well in containers. A surprising number of different vegetables will grow in pots too, especially if given a large enough container. Tomatoes, courgettes, carrots, leeks, potatoes and runner beans are just a few of the vegetables that will thrive in a good-sized pot.

From early April, you can start sowing vegetables and herbs that tolerate the cold – such as radishes, lettuce and chives – in pots outdoors. More tender species, such as cucumber, tomatoes, sweet pepper or basil, should be raised from seed indoors and only planted outdoors in late May. Alternatively buy healthy young plants from a nursery.

A sunny spot is best

When choosing vegetables for pots and planters, go for compact-growing early varieties. They need plenty of sunlight, and growing them successfully on balconies and patios depends on their position. You can even grow heat-loving plants like aubergines in an open and sunny position, as long as it's sheltered.

Mediterranean herbs, such as rosemary, sage and thyme, also need plenty of sun while others, like chervil and parsley, prefer moist, partial shade. Stand the pots in a well-ventilated spot so that rainwater does not remain too long on leaves, causing mildew.

Beans are easy to grow in a pot. Choose low-growing varieties or stake taller beans.

Soil and water

When choosing a container, make sure it's big enough to accommodate the eventual size of the plant, and that it has sufficient drainage. You can use any potting compost – many contain water-retaining granules and most are already nutrient-enriched. You can also buy compost specially formulated for herbs, which do not thrive in rich soil.

Water plants in the morning and take care to keep the leaves as dry as possible. Leaves need to be able to dry off before nightfall in order to minimise the risk of disease. With tomatoes, sweet peppers and other fruiting vegetables, it is important to water around the plant bases and not over the top of the leaves. Rather than little and often, it's better to water generously, but less frequently. Feed your vegetables with an organic fertiliser every three or four weeks for a bountiful harvest.

Feed water to the roots of newly planted vegetables in pots by taking a plastic bottle with the base cut off and pushing it, upside-down, into the compost near the bottom of the plant. Fill with water; this will seep out gradually, keeping the compost moist.

Container-grown lettuce

1 Line a wooden box with plastic sheeting, trimming the top flush with the top of the box. Punch small holes in the bottom for drainage.

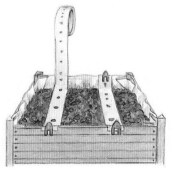

2 Fill the box with compost and put in your seeds. You can buy ready-made seed tapes that contain the correct number of seeds, spaced appropriately. Press the seeds down carefully, cover with a thin layer of soil and then water.

3 You should soon be able to pick the first leaves of 'cut-and-come-again' varieties. Cut or pick the outer leaves only of frilly types of lettuce such as Lollo Rosso, leaving the heart intact, and the plants will keep on growing, providing you with more leaves.

Freshly picked fruit has more flavour than anything you can buy in a shop. You can grow delicious apples and plums to eat straight from the tree, or a range of berries perfect for jams and baking. With clever planning and the right varieties, you can create a productive, easy-care fruit garden.

For a low-maintenance fruit garden, grow primarily hardy fruit trees with basic requirements in terms of soil and site. A sunny site and a humus-rich garden soil are all most fruit trees and bushes need. Apple trees thrive practically anywhere, but do not like overly warm and dry places, while sour Morello cherries do not like wet soils.

If you choose low-growing columnar varieties – also known as ballerina or minarette trees – and espalier trees that you train over a wall, the crop will be easily accessible, and even such small trees may produce more fruit than you can use. In a small garden, plant an early and a late fruiting tree side by side, so that fruit crops over a longer period. Minarette fruit trees do not form a large crown, so you can grow strawberries or lettuces around the base.

Low-maintenance bushes

For delicious homemade pies and crumbles, fruit bushes such as blackcurrants and gooseberries are a good choice. They don't

A group of standard redcurrants can produce a bumper crop of fruit; an underplanting of strawberries increases the harvest.

Gooseberries are an easy fruit to grow and there are dessert varieties available which do not need to be cooked to be eaten

take up much room and provide pickings even in their first year. Raspberry canes are really easy to grow, and if you choose an autumn fruiting variety you can enjoy succulent fruits right into October. If you like making jam, loganberries or tayberries (a blackberry and raspberry hybrid) are well worth growing.

Strawberries into autumn

There is space for a crop of strawberries in even the smallest gardens. Most varieties form numerous runners and will spread to produce an abundant harvest: choose from 'Elvira' (an early cropper), 'Hapil' (mid-season fruit), 'Maxim' (late) and 'Bolero' (which bears fruits all season). Cut back the foliage after picking.

Alpine strawberries, which produce tiny red berries from June until autumn, don't form runners and therefore make excellent edging plants for a flower or vegetable bed.

Lay a straw mulch around and beneath your strawberry plants to help deter slugs and prevent botrytis – a fungal disease common in strawberries.

A decorative fruit bed

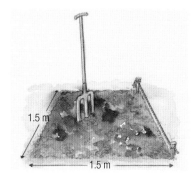

1.5 m

1.5 m

1 Mark out a bed measuring 1.5m by 1.5m. Break up the soil, dig in a bucketful of well rotted manure and fork over the soil further until crumbly. Rake the surface smooth.

2 Plant a small mature currant or gooseberry standard in the centre. Hammer in a sturdy stake the length of the trunk alongside it. Secure the trunk to the stake.

3 At the base of the standard, plant four strawberry plants and four perennial herbs such as thyme, sage, garlic and chives. These will help to keep pests at bay and will attract beneficial insects. Fill any gaps with flowers and lettuce.

Fruit trees come in all shapes and sizes and can be grown in many different situations, so there is one suitable for every garden. Once established, fruit trees usually crop reliably and need little maintenance beyond the occasional prune and monitoring for pests or diseases.

Low-growing fruit trees are best for most domestic gardens. Make sure that you check that the tree you are buying is suitable for your plot – or you could end up with a monster. With a crown not exceeding 2.5m in diameter, and a trunk height of about 60cm, apples and pears sold as dwarf or spindle bushes are easy to look after and harvest. There are small cultivars of cherry trees, plums and damsons with a trunk height of 60cm and a 3m wide crown.

The crowns of apricot and peach trees usually measure about 5m across. These fruit trees prefer warmer spots, but both can be trained as an espalier against a sheltered house wall.

Planting fruit trees

Fruit trees are sold as bare-root, root-ball or container-grown plants. Bare-root and root-ball trees are best planted in the cooler months of spring or autumn; container-grown trees can be planted out all year round as long as the ground is not frozen. Whatever the root type, soak the roots in a bucket of water while you prepare the hole. This should be about 1m wide and 60cm deep so that there is plenty of room to spread out the roots.

Trim the roots of bare-root trees a little before planting. Always plant the tree so that the grafting site, which is visible as a thickening in the trunk, remains above

There's an apple tree available to suit any size of garden. **Plums are delicious eaten** straight from the tree (below).

Prune established
trees lightly

Prune young
trees hard

Use an extendable picking tool to harvest the topmost fruit.

ground. Tread down the soil around the trunk to firm it and tie the tree to a stake so that it will withstand strong winds. Certain fruit trees, like some apples and pears, need to be planted near a compatible tree to ensure pollination (see page 87).

Pruning fruit trees

Immediately after planting, remove competing branches, leaving only the central branch and a maximum of four strong 'leader' branches. Over the next few years, pruning should be carried out to prevent branches overlapping and getting in each other's way, and to stop the crown becoming congested. This will also help to shape the crown nicely.

During subsequent years, continue pruning to keep the crown in shape, thin out overcrowded branches and ensure a good yield. Always remove any stray shoots sprouting from the base of the trunk along with any long 'water' shoots on the branches that take nutrients from the tree without producing any fruit. Cut old fruit branches back to the point where young shoots are growing, which will in turn set fruit. If necessary, prune large branches right back to the trunk.

Aphid deterrents

Creating a circular bed around a young fruit tree promotes healthy growth. Remove weeds, grass or other plant matter from an area measuring about 1.5m across around the tree. Mulch the bed with compost in autumn, then sow it with nasturtiums in spring to provide shade for the soil and prevent it from drying out. Nasturtiums are a magnet for blackfly so will help to keep the tree free of this pest. Put up nesting boxes to attract blue tits. The birds feed on insects living in the branches. Alternatively, hang a clay plant pot upside down in the branches and fill it with straw to attract earwigs, which also eat aphids.

Fruit bushes and low-growing fruit trees can create a pretty and productive hedge. Use them to divide up areas within your garden – you will want to have access to both sides of the hedge if you are going to enjoy all the fruits of your labour!

Soft fruit bushes are ideal for making a hedge, as are low-growing apple varieties. Most soft fruit bushes will thrive in almost any site, whether in full sun or partial shade, as long as the soil is rich in humus and nutrients. They produce their sweetest fruit, however, when grown in a sunny position.

Planting currants

Depending on the variety, currant bushes, which can reach a height of 2m, bear fruit from June to August. Plant them in autumn, so that the plants have time to become established by spring. Give them plenty of space and encourage them to produce as many new roots as possible by planting them slightly deeper than they were growing at the nursery. Water throughly after planting, and then prune the stems to stimulate growth (see above right). In spring, mulch the soil around the plants with straw, leaves or bark.

From then on, prune currants between November and March. Red and white currants set their fruit on two or three-year-old wood, blackcurrants on the previous season's growth. The bushes of red and white currants need to be airy, so prune the centres of established bushes, leaving between eight and 12 stems (just pruning the tips of these). Cut back side shoots to one bud.

Blackcurrants also need light and air but require more vigorous pruning to achieve a good crop. Cut back a third to a quarter of all fruited branches on established bushes, leaving about eight healthy stems.

A hedge of raspberries produces an abundance of luscious fruit, ripe and ready to pick during summer.

Planting fruit bushes

1 Before planting, soak the roots for an hour in a bucket of water. Dig a hole deep enough for the plant to sit at a lower depth than it was in its container or at the nursery. Put a layer of well-rotted compost in the base of the hole before planting.

2 Backfill around the plant with soil and firm it down well. Mound up the soil so that it forms a ridge around the plant about 15cm from the stem; water well. The ridge of soil should retain the water, allowing it to seep into the soil around the plant.

3 Cut down raspberry and blackberry canes to a bud 25–30cm from the base. Cut back all stems of blackcurrants to a bud 3–5cm above the base. Cut back all stems of red and white currants by a third and gooseberry branches by half.

Raspberries and blackberries

Loose soil with a high humus content is ideal for raspberries and blackberries, and though they do best in a sunny site, they will tolerate partial shade. If you construct a simple wire framework along your boundary, you will be able to tie in the fruit canes to the wires. Different varieties of raspberry produce fruit at different times; some even produce two crops, one in summer and one in autumn.

Thornless cultivars of the vigorous blackberry make harvesting much easier. They are less hardy than the wild variety and need a sheltered spot as they can be damaged by frost. Blackberries and raspberries fruit on young wood, so cut back shoots that have borne fruit right to the ground after the fruit has been picked.

Plant a raspberry hedge in autumn, leaving a 50cm gap between each plant. To encourage growth, add plenty of well-rotted compost to the planting holes. Ensure that the leaf buds on the roots, which go on to produce new canes, are about 5cm beneath the soil. Water the planting site and mulch with well-rotted manure. When the canes shoot up, tie them to the wire frame.

Stretch wires between stakes to make a framework to support young raspberry canes as they grow into a hedge.

Just because space is at a premium there is no reason to go without home-grown fresh fruit. Soft fruit bushes and even fruit trees can be grown in tubs and pots on a balcony or patio. Look out for smaller growing varieties to make the most of the space you have.

There are many varieties of fruit that can be grown in pots. Berry bushes are easy to grow in large containers and look especially decorative as single-stem plants; even fruit-trees grafted onto a slow-growing rootstock can be grown in containers. And heat lovers, like peaches and apricots, often do better grown on a balcony or patio than in the open garden.

Place fruit grown in containers in a sunny spot, or somewhere that, at the very least, receives a minimum of three hours of sunlight each day. Choose a container suited to the size of plant with ample room left for growth. Use ready-mixed potting compost or a mixture of garden soil and compost. As with all pots, a drainage layer of pebbles or broken flower pots in the bottom of the container is essential for preventing the accumulation of water.

Nurturing a good crop

With a little care, it's easy to produce a worthwhile harvest from container-grown fruit trees. If there is any chance of frost after a fruit tree has blossomed, wrap some horticultural fleece around the crown to protect the blooms from damage. Fruit trees need plenty of water, particularly when they are flowering. In spring, feed the plants with a suitable slow-release fertiliser, and once again in early summer.

Don't feed fruit trees after July or they will continue to form new shoots well into autumn and these will be susceptible to the first frosts in November. Pruning requirements are minimal – just an occasional thinning out, as well as the removal of dead or damaged shoots, or those that have failed to fruit (assuming the plant fruits on new rather than old wood).

Strawberries make perfect pot plants; repot every year and renew plants every three years to ensure a good crop in your container.

Care for containers

Hardy fruit trees usually have no problem surviving winter outdoors, even those grown in tubs. Cluster them in groups or move single specimens into a sheltered spot, such as close to a wall or beneath an overhang. If very harsh conditions with prolonged frost are forecast, stand the containers on pieces of polystyrene and wrap them in fleece to protect the roots from freezing. Don't let the soil get too wet or too dry.

After two or three years, if the plant has outgrown its tub and the soil is compacted and depleted of nutrients, repot into a container that is only slightly larger (if the roots remain slightly restricted the plant will put more energy into producing fruit rather than growing roots), or renew the top layer of compost, preferably in the spring (see pages 58–59).

Choosing trees

Many fruit trees – particularly apples – are not self-pollinating, and only produce fruit if another variety is growing nearby. In order to ensure a good crop, two different varieties should be sited near each other if possible. Some nurseries sell duo or 'family' trees, in which two or more varieties are grafted onto the same trunk. This allows mutual pollination, guaranteeing a harvest of both varieties of fruit.

A great choice for a balcony is the columnar fruit tree – sometimes called ballerina or minarette – in which short, fruit-bearing side shoots grow around a strong vertical central trunk. These rarely grow more than 30cm wide, and even after five years seldom exceed 2m in height. If, however, you prefer a small tree with a round crown, choose apple, cherry and pear trees grafted onto dwarf-growing rootstocks. These small specimens grow no taller than 1.5m but bear normal-sized fruit.

A dwarf cherry tree in a pot looks beautiful when in bloom and is easier to protect from birds when in fruit.

Pest and disease control

It's hard to avoid pests and diseases in the vegetable patch but their presence is often due to a few simple cultivation errors. You can limit these problems by choosing suitably resistant varieties and by adopting a system of companion planting.

Good, nutritious soil and enough water, light and air are vital for healthy plant growth. But the varieties you choose will also have a bearing on whether or not your vegetables will be attacked by pests or harmed by disease. For example, summer varieties planted outside in spring always do badly and have little resistance to attack. And conversely, outdoor varieties grown under glass often succumb to pests and diseases. Always choose the appropriate varieties for specific growing environments, and look for cultivars that are resistant to fungal, bacterial or viral infections as well as to common garden pests.

Make a slug-pub by placing a flower pot over a container of beer; slugs and snails crawl through the drainage hole of the pot to get to the beer. They cannot climb back out and drown in the beer.

Plants to help one another

Companion planting makes the most of the beneficial effects that plants can have on each other – and their deterrent effect on pests. Aromatic compounds in roots, leaves and flowers or secretions from parts of some plants can help to repel many common pests. Growing carrots with leeks, garlic or onions is a tried and tested combination, with these companions affording each other mutual protection against carrot fly and

Protect cabbages and other leafy vegetables from pests by covering with a fine gauze, pegged into the ground around the plants.

Ideal companions and planting combinations to avoid

Vegetables	Good neighbours	Bad neighbours
Peas	Carrots, cucumbers, kohlrabi, lettuce, courgettes, radishes.	Beans, potatoes, tomatoes, onions, leeks.
Cucumbers	Peas, kohlrabi, leeks, dill, caraway.	Tomatoes, radishes, potatoes.
Potatoes	Spinach.	Tomatoes.
Cabbages	Dill, coriander, caraway, butterhead lettuce, chicory, peas, beans, potatoes.	Strawberries, onions, mustard, garlic.
Butterhead lettuce	Dill, cress, radishes, leeks, carrots, tomatoes, cabbages, onions.	Parsley, celery.
Carrots	Onions, leeks, garlic, Swiss chard.	Beetroot.
Tomatoes	Parsley, lettuce, leeks, cabbages.	Peas, potatoes, fennel, cucumbers.
Onions	Carrots, winter savory, dill, strawberries, lettuce.	Beans, peas, brassicas.

onion fly. When planted between strawberries and vegetables, onions and garlic also help to protect the other plants against fungal infections.

Strong-smelling winter savory protects dwarf beans against blackfly, whereas nasturtiums help to protect tomatoes and fruit trees from greenfly and the woolly apple aphid. When planted among vegetables, secretions from the roots of pot marigolds (*Calendula officinalis*) and French marigolds (*Tagetes patula*) help to deter eelworms, which damage leaves.

Planting celery between cabbage plants drives away cabbage white butterflies, so that they look elsewhere for a place to lay their eggs. And the aromatic leaves of sage also deter cabbage whites, as well as being offputting to snails and ants.

Not only do companion plants protect against pests, but they reduce weed growth, too. Because deep-rooting plants are planted alongside shallow-rooting plants, and compact plants with broad leaves are grown alongside thin-leafed plants, there is simply less room for weeds to take hold.

Other organic tips

Use netting, horticultural fleece and collars to keep vegetable fly, leek moth and cabbage fly away from your vegetable patch. An infusion of horsetail (*Equisetum arvense*) also helps prevent fungal infections. Just boil up two dessertspoons of the dried weed in two litres of water, leave to infuse for 15 minutes, cool and then strain. Every two or three weeks, on a sunny morning, spray the infusion over the plants and the soil.

Remember to rotate crops in the vegetable patch (see page 74). Otherwise, if you grow vegetables in the same position year after year, certain pests and diseases will become firmly established, lying dormant in the soil between growing seasons.

A–Z of
easy-care
plants

A selection of some of the easiest garden plants to grow, this directory gives you information on the perfect situation and ideal growing conditions for a wide range of different species. It will help you to pick the right plant for the right place and thus save both time and money.

Light requirements

- ○ **Sunny:** the whole day in sun
- ◑ **Partial sun:** sunny but no full midday sun
- ◐ **Partial shade:** half the day in sun or beneath a light tree canopy
- ● **Shade:** the whole day without direct sun

Plant size

- ▲ **Average height** including flowers
- ▶ **Average spread** when grown in isolation

Water requirements

- ◆ **Thirsty:** do not allow to dry out, must be watered a lot
- ◑ **Average:** can be dry for a short time, water moderately
- ◌ **Little:** can withstand drought at times, must not be watered too much

Allium

Allium species and cultivars

| ○ | ▲ 1.7m | ▶ 1m | ◌ |

The ornamental onions are grown for their showy flowerheads held on erect stems. *A. giganteum* is perhaps the most eye-catching,

with large flowerheads on tall stems.
Flower Spherical flowerheads in white, yellow or shades of pink, purple and blue appear in early to mid summer.
Maintenance In autumn plant bulbs 10–20cm deep and at least 25cm apart. Deadhead to prevent prolific self-seeding. Leave bulbs undisturbed for several years. For propagation purposes, lift and divide after flowering.

Alyssum

Alyssum montanum

| ○ | ▲ 20cm | ▶ 30cm | ◌ |

Spreading mats of evergreen foliage become smothered in yellow flowers in summer. The plants can be used to soften the lines of a raised bed: position them at the front and they will tumble over the edge. Ideal in rockeries and sink gardens.
Flower Fragrant, deep yellow flowers are carried in abundant clusters from late spring to mid summer.
Maintenance Trim back lightly after flowering to encourage bushy growth.
Tip Established plants often self-seed freely.

Apple

Malus x *domestica* cultivars

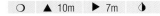

○ ▲ 10m ▶ 7m ◐

Apples are the most widely grown fruit tree in Britain because they are hardy and easy to maintain. A huge choice of varieties offers fruiting from August to November.

Flower Clusters of five-petalled white or pinkish flowers in spring.

Maintenance Apply a compound fertiliser in late winter. Keep well watered. A few weeks after petal fall, thin young fruit to one or two per cluster. Prune in mid to late winter.

Harvest Autumn. Wait for fruit to ripen on the tree before picking.

Astilbe

Astilbe species and cultivars

◐ – ● ▲ 1.2m ▶ 75cm ●

A gift in a tricky situation, astilbes thrive in damp shade. There are many easy varieties to choose from, all bearing tall, fluffy plumes of summer flowers above ferny foliage.

Flower Spires of deep red flowers appear in mid to late summer.

Maintenance Divide every four years to maintain vigour.

Tip Apply a thick mulch in spring to prevent plants from drying out.

Aubrieta

Aubrieta cultivars

○ ▲ 15cm ▶ 60cm ◐

Compact cushions of grey-green foliage become smothered in brightly coloured flowers in spring. They make ideal rockery plants and will grow on dry sunny walls or in the cracks between paving.

Flower Elongating clusters of pink, purple or blue cross-shaped flowers are carried throughout the spring.

Maintenance Divide plants in late summer or early autumn.

Tip There are numerous cultivars to choose from, including 'Belisha Beacon' (bright rose-red flowers), 'Doctor Mules' (rich violet flowers) and 'Triumphant' (blue flowers).

Ballerina apple

Malus x *domestica* cultivars

○ ▲ 2m ▶ 40cm ◐

This compact tree is the ultimate in care-free gardening since it requires little pruning and the fruits are easy to pick. Its vertical habit with few side shoots allows it to be sited in small gardens, borders and even tubs. Cultivars include 'Bolero' (green) and 'Flamenco' (red).

Flower Clusters of five-petalled white or pinkish flowers in spring.

Maintenance Care is the same as for all apple trees. Minimal pruning is required: cut back any side shoots to two buds in winter.

Harvest Autumn, when fruit is ripe.

Barberry
Berberis thunbergii

○ – ◑ ▲ 1.8m ▶ 2.4m ◇

Colourful leaves, flowers and berries make *B. thunbergii* both versatile and excellent value. The densely packed reddish brown thorny branches of this neat, compact deciduous shrub form an impenetrable hedge. The cultivar 'Pow-wow' has bright yellow leaves that gradually turn green; 'Silver Beauty' has white and bluish green variegated leaves.

Flower/Fruit Pale, straw-coloured flowers suffused with red in spring. Small red berries in autumn.

Maintenance Encourage strong new growth by cutting out a few old stems each year. Trim barberry hedges once a year in late summer or late autumn after the berries have fallen.

Tip Position barberry plants in full sun for the best leaf coloration.

Blackberry
Rubus fruticosus

○ ▲ 2m ◐

With pretty flowers and autumn leaf colour, blackberries make an attractive display on an archway. The long, rambling canes also bear an abundance of plump purple-black berries in autumn.

Flower Clusters of white flowers in late spring and summer.

Maintenance Train canes between pairs of wires. Growth and fruiting follows a two-year cycle, so canes that have finished fruiting should be cut out at ground level in late autumn.

Harvest From late summer to early autumn, depending on variety.

Blackthorn, sloe
Prunus spinosa

○ – ◑ ▲ 6m ▶ 4m ◇

A hardy native shrub, frequently seen wild in hedgerows. Its densely branching habit and stout thorns form a suitably deterring barrier and make it an ideal hedging plant.

Flower/Fruit Small white flowers appear in early spring and give way to small blue-black fruits in autumn.

Maintenance Trim in early summer to maintain size and shape.

Tip The fruit may be used to make sloe gin.

Box
Buxus sempervirens

○ – ● ▲ 3m ▶ 3m ◐

Small evergreen leaves, dense growth and tolerance of frequent clipping make box an ideal hedging plant. It will grow in shade or

full sun, so can be utilised anywhere in the garden, the dark green foliage contrasting beautifully with flowers and gravel paths.

Flower Inconspicuous.

Maintenance Clip hedges two or three times a year.

Tip Can be grown for topiary.

Bugle
Ajuga reptans

A low, spreading evergreen plant that provides effective ground cover in any damp, lightly shaded spot. During late spring and early summer it is adorned with lovely blue flowers.

Flower Short blue flower spikes appear from spring to early summer.

Maintenance If it spreads outside its allotted space you can take brutal action without harming the plant. Slice through clumps with a spade in spring.

Tip Some cultivars have attractive foliage.

The cultivar 'Burgundy Glow' has creamy green and red leaves; 'Atropurpurea' has dark purple leaves.

Busy lizzie
Impatiens walleriana

One of the most free-flowering bedding plants for shady sites, busy lizzie is a popular pot plant. Its many hybrids can be grown in containers indoors and outside. It is a perennial, but is normally treated as half-hardy annual. It is also a useful bedding plant for shady sites.

Flower White, pink, red, violet, orange or two-toned flowers appear from summer through to autumn.

Maintenance Plants can be overwintered under cover.

Calamagrostis
Calamagrostis x acutiflora

Calamagrostis, a medium-sized grass, bears narrow, long-living, purple-green plumes on tall stems. It is a rhizomatous perennial with mid green leaves that form tufts.

Flower Purple-green plumes in early summer gradually turn brown.

Maintenance None needed.

Tip The cultivar 'Karl Foerster' has red-bronze heads that fade to buff.

California poppy

Eschscholzia californica

○ ▲ 60cm ▶ 40cm ◑

An easy-to-grow hardy annual for poor, dry soil. It needs full sun, however, for its flowers to open fully. The bright poppy flowers are carried on slender stems well above the finely divided blue-green leaves.
Flower Yellow and orange flowers from early summer to mid autumn.
Maintenance None needed.
Tip Deadhead to prolong flowering.

Carex

Carex elata 'Aurea'

○–◐ ▲ 60cm ▶ 1m ◑

Plant this sedge for a splash of intense colour. The leaves, which form dense mounds, are bright yellow and narrowly edged with green. Like all the sedges it grows well in sun or shade but needs a moist soil.
Flower Dark brown flower spikes appear in early summer.
Maintenance Divide plants in spring or early summer.
Tip The plant is an attractive addition to a bog garden.

Catmint

Nepeta x faassenii

○–◐ ▲ 60cm ▶ 60cm ◐

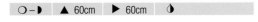

Catmint adds a gentle touch as an edging plant with a soft haze of light-blue flowers

against silvery grey leaves. It will also droop attractively over the edge of a pot.
Flower Pale lavender flowers appear during the summer.
Maintenance Divide in early spring.
Tip Its aromatic leaves and flowers attract bees into the garden.

Chives

Allium schoenoprasum

○–◐ ▲ 30cm ◑

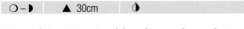

Grow chives in mixed borders, where their mauve-pink spherical flowers will add colour in summer, year after year. The hollow, cylindrical leaves are harvested and have a mild onion flavour.
Maintenance Sow seeds outside in spring. Divide clumps every three or four years during autumn.
Harvest March to October.
Tip Remove any flowerheads before they open if you want a plentiful and regular supply of leaves.

Clematis

Clematis montana

○–◐ ▲ 6m ▶ 3m ◑

Rightly known as the queen of climbers, clematis brightens up a wall or trellis with sumptuous colour. There are hundreds to

choose from; *C. montana* is particularly easy
to grow. It flowers in profusion in late
spring, creating a display that can last three
to four weeks.
Flower White or pink open flowers with
prominent stamens in late spring.
Maintenance Cut back overgrown plants
after flowering.
Tip The cultivar 'Elizabeth' has particularly
fine pink flowers; the species and the form
grandiflora bear white blooms.

Climbing hydrangea

Hydrangea anomala spp. *petiolaris*

 ◑ – ● ▲ 10m ▶ 5m ◐

Climbing hydrangeas support themselves via
aerial roots and do not need tying in. Use
them to clothe a wall with greenery and
adorn it with white blooms. Avoid planting
against a south-facing wall.
Flower Large, flat, cream and white lacy
flowerheads cover the plant in summer.
Maintenance Prune only to keep plant close
to wall. Pruning not necessary when grown
on trees.
Tip An alternative climbing species is the
evergreen *H. serratifolia*.

Columbine

Aquilegia vulgaris

◑ – ◗ ▲ 80cm ▶ 40cm ◐

Dainty, nodding flowers are held on slender
stems above lacy foliage on this easily grown
plant. Native to British woodland, it thrives
in dappled shade and humus-rich soil,
although it will tolerate drier soils. It flowers
freely, seeding itself widely.
Flower Blue, purple, reddish purple, white
or pink flowers in early summer.
Maintenance None needed.
Tip Recommended cultivars include 'Nivea'
(white flowers) and *A. vulgaris* var. *stellata*
'Nora Barlow' (pompom-like pink flowers
flecked with lime green and white).

Common or cherry laurel

Prunus laurocerasus

○ – ● ▲ 8m ▶ 4m ◐

This attractive vigorous large evergreen
shrub or small tree has glossy mid-green
leaves and bears attractive upright spikes of
flowers in spring. It is robust and trouble
free and grows to the perfect height for a
screen or windbreak. The cultivar 'Otto
Luyken' can be grown as low hedging or in
a small border.
Flower/Fruit White flower spikes appear in
mid spring followed by a profusion of black
fruits in early autumn.
Maintenance Generally trouble free, it needs
only an occasional trim to keep it in shape.
Tip Will tolerate shade, but does not thrive
on chalky soils.

Cosmos

Cosmos bipinnatus

| ○ | ▲ 1.2m | ▶ 80cm | ◐ |

Brightly coloured, saucer-shaped flowers are carried on tall, slender stems above ferny foliage. The overall appearance is delicate and refined, yet this bushy annual is robust and easy to grow. It is excellent in areas of poor, dry soil, readily flowering where other plants may have trouble. There are several varieties to choose from, including 'Sonata White', which has shorter stems and white petals surrounding the yellow centre.

Flower Saucer-shaped flowers with yellow centres and rose, crimson, pink or white petals appear from mid summer to autumn.

Maintenance None needed.

Tip Deadhead regularly to encourage the production of more flowers.

Cotoneaster

Cotoneaster adpressus

| ○ – ◐ | ▲ 30cm | ▶ 1m | ○ |

The cotoneaster is an undemanding, low, spreading shrub that is ideal for ground

cover. Its dull green leaves turn a striking scarlet shade in autumn.

Flower/Fruit Pinkish white flowers in summer are followed by red berries.

Maintenance No need to prune.

Cranesbill

Geranium species and cultivars

| ◐ – ◑ | ▲ 1.5m | ▶ 1.5m | ◐ |

Geraniums are easy-to-grow perennials that are suitable for a wide range of situations. There are tall-growing varieties that reach over 1m in height and low-growing plants that reach up to 30cm. Many have a wide spread, making them ideal for covering a large area.

Flower Ranging through purple, pink, blue, and white with several shades and different markings in between.

Maintenance Divide clump-forming plants in late summer or spring. Cut back spring-flowering varieties after they bloom to encourage a second show.

Tip *G.* x *magnificum*, *G. sanguineum* and *G. macrorrhizum* (below) are ideal species for ground cover; the variety 'Wargrave Pink' bears abundant creamy pink flowers.

Creeping Jenny

Lysimachia nummularia

| ○ – ● | ▲ 10cm | ▶ 1m | ◐ |

A rampantly spreading evergreen perennial, use Creeping Jenny as ground cover in shady places. Its prostrate mats of bright

green foliage become studded with pretty yellow flowers in summer.

Flower Bright yellow flowers appear during early summer.

Maintenance Divide plants in autumn to control spread.

Tip 'Aurea' has golden leaves.

Crocus

Crocus species and cultivars

○ – ◑   ▲ 20cm   ▶ 5cm   ◐

There are numerous crocus species and varieties to choose from. The early flowering *C. tommasinianus* increases rapidly and is good for naturalising in grass.

Flower Honey-scented flowers in white or shades of yellow, purple and blue appear in late winter and early spring.

Maintenance In autumn plant corms 5cm deep at 10cm intervals.

Daffodil

Narcissus cultivars

○ – ◗   ▲ 60cm   ▶ 50cm   ○

One of the best known flowers of spring, daffodils are easy to grow and there is a wide variety to choose from. They can be grown in a range of settings from natural drifts in a lawn to pots on a windowsill.

Flower The spring flowers come in white and shades of yellow, orange-red or pink; many varieties are bicoloured.

Maintenance In autumn plant bulbs 5–15cm deep and 5–20cm apart.

Tip The cultivar 'Geranium' is one of many sweetly fragrant daffodils.

Day lily

Hemerocallis cultivars

○ – ◗   ▲ 1.1m   ▶ 60cm   ◐

The day lily's brilliantly coloured exotic flowers are available in an ever-increasing

range of shapes and colours. They create a majestic summer display against a backdrop of strap-shaped, arching leaves.

Flower Pure white, orange, yellow, striped, red and much more.

Maintenance Divide in late summer to maintain vigour.

Tip The flowers last one day only but are continually replaced; deadhead daily for the best show.

Dogwood
Cornus alba

 ◐ – ◑ ▲ 3m ▶ 6m ◐

Grown for its flowers, foliage and brilliant winter stem colour, the red-barked dogwood has year-round appeal. It is a vigorous plant and regular pruning encourages the production of numerous crimson stems. The foliage turns crimson and purple in autumn.

Flower/Fruit Flattened clusters of small yellow-white flowers in early summer, followed by pale blue-white berries.

Maintenance To maintain good colour, cut back to the ground every two or three years in late spring.

Tip The slightly shorter cultivar 'Aurea' (below) has golden yellow leaves in summer.

Dotted loosestrife
Lysimachia punctata

 ◐ – ◗ ▲ 2m ▶ 60cm ◐

Tall spires of bright yellow flowers add interest to the back of a border. Loosestrife needs fairly moist soil and will thrive if

placed around a pond or beside a stream. Its rampant habit is best suited to wild or cottage gardens where it will grow into broad swathes.

Flower Bright yellow star-shaped flowers appear in summer.

Maintenance Keep invasiveness in check by deadheading so that it cannot self-seed and by cutting clumps back ruthlessly in spring.

Dwarf French bean
Phaseolus vulgaris var. *nanus*

 ◯ ▲ 50cm ◇

A low-growing bean that does not require tying to supports. This variety is small enough to be grown in tubs and containers, where its heavy crop of slender beans can be easily accessed.

Maintenance Sow outdoors in late May or June in rows 45cm apart at 10cm intervals for easier picking.

Harvest As soon as first pods develop – from seven or eight weeks after sowing.

Echinacea
Echinacea purpurea

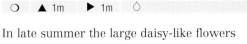
○ ▲ 1m ▶ 1m ◇

In late summer the large daisy-like flowers of echinacea (above) make a bold addition to a sunny border. The flowers are long-lasting. Herbaceous perennials, they are ideal for dry borders.

Flower White to purple flowers with an orange-brown centre appear from late summer into autumn.

Maintenance Divide in autumn or spring. Deadhead to prolong flowering.

Tip The flowers are good for both cutting and drying.

Elder
Sambucus nigra

○ – ◗ ▲ 7m ▶ 5m ◇

A shrub of wild hedgerows, common elder makes a trouble-free addition to the garden,

although it is prone to be rather invasive. There are several cultivars available with attractive foliage that make better garden subjects, including 'Aurea' with golden foliage and the small, slow-growing 'Pulverulenta' with white-mottled leaves.

Flower/Fruit Flat, creamy white clusters of small, delicately scented flowers appear in early summer followed by bunches of small black berries.

Maintenance Prune stems back to ground level in winter to prevent the plant becoming straggly and outgrowing its space.

Tip The flowers and berries can be used to make wine and cordial.

Epimedium
Epimedium grandiflorum

◗ – ● ▲ 25cm ▶ 20cm ◐

A clump-forming, herbaceous plant, grown for its superb foliage and intriguing, long-spurred flowers. The apple-green leaves flush bronze in spring and again in autumn. A shade-loving plant, the ideal location is in a semi-woodland position with plenty of humus in the soil.

Flower White, pink, violet or rose-red flowers bloom in spring and early summer.

Maintenance Divide plants in autumn or early spring.

Tip Recommended varieties include 'Nanum' (pale purple flowers), 'Rose Queen' (deep pink flowers and copper-tinged young leaves) and 'White Queen' (pure white flowers and bronze-tinged young leaves).

Firethorn
Pyracantha cultivars

○ – ◑   ▲ 3m   ▶ 2m   ◊

The firethorns are favoured for their glossy evergreen leaves and sumptuous autumn displays of brilliantly coloured berries. They can be easily trained up a wall and make dense, colourful hedging.

Flower/Fruit Frothy clusters of tiny white flowers appear in early summer, followed by berries that persist well into winter.

Maintenance Prune just before flowering to encourage a good show of berries later on.

Tip Beware of the shrub's long, sharp thorns when pruning.

Flowering plum
Prunus cerasifera

○ – ●   ▲ 9m   ▶ 4m   ◐

The flowering plum is grown for its dazzling spring display, with clouds of exquisite blossom. It is easy to grow, requiring just a trim in late summer after flowering.

Flower/Fruit Small pinkish white flowers appear in early spring, followed by yellow or red fruits.

Maintenance Give it a light trim to shape in late summer.

Tip Allow for its spreading habit.

Flowering quince
Chaenomeles speciosa

○ – ◗   ▲ 1.5m   ▶ 1.5m   ◊

A decorative shrub for a border or low ornamental hedge. The flowers are profuse in spring, but fairly short-lived. After flowering the plant can be used as a natural support for climbing annuals.

Flower/Fruit Bowl-shaped, predominantly red flowers are borne in early spring and followed by fragrant, green, apple-shaped fruits in autumn.

Maintenance Cut back shoots that have flowered in May. Grows best trained against a sunny wall.

Tip For reliable flower colour choose a cultivar such as 'Geisha Girl' (above).

Foam flower
Tiarella cordifolia

◗ – ●   ▲ 30cm   ▶ 1m   ◐

This species of foam flower produces masses of spires of white frothy blossom in spring. Its pale green leaves are shallowly lobed and develop a bronze tint in winter. It is mat-forming, providing ground cover in damp, shady places.

Flower Spires of tiny white flowers appear in late spring and early summer.
Maintenance Spreads quickly and may need cutting back to control growth in spring.

Forsythia
Forsythia x intermedia

The brilliant yellow flowers of forsythia herald the spring. This vigorous hybrid is hardy and easily grown. It can be used as a specimen shrub or to cover a wall or trellis at the back of a border.
Flower Golden yellow flowers from early to mid spring.
Maintenance To avoid straggly growth, prune flowered shoots to within two buds of old wood. Grows well in any soil in sun or partial shade.
Tip Cutting back hard limits size, without causing damage.

Globe thistle
Echinops ritro

A stately plant that bears large spherical flowerheads on stout stems (above right). The thistle-like, spiky leaves are divided, greyish green to dark green. It is a useful plant for the poorest and driest of soils, where its deep blue or purplish flowers will bring splashes of intense colour. The slightly taller hybrid *E.* 'Nivalis' has greyish-white globular flowerheads on grey stems with greyer leaves.
Flower Dark steel-blue flowerheads from mid summer to early autumn.
Maintenance Divide in spring or autumn.
Tip Cut the flowerheads before they are fully opened and dry for use in flower arrangements.

Grape
Vitis coignetiae

Ornamental grape vines are at their best in autumn when they cover pergolas and trellises with colourful foliage and fruit. This species is a good choice for poor soil, which will bring out the best display of autumn colour in spectacular shades of yellow, orange-red and purple-crimson. It is best grown over trees or old buildings.
Fruit Clusters of inedible black grapes with an attractive purple bloom hang decoratively in autumn.
Maintenance Thin out old growth during late summer.
Tip Choose a south-facing site.

Grape hyacinth
Muscari species and cultivars

This plant gets its name from the clusters of globular flowers that resemble a bunch of grapes. Looks attractive planted among daffodils. Best in a sunny border although will tolerate light shade.

Flower Purple-blue flowers in mid spring.
Maintenance In August plant 5–10cm deep and 5–10cm apart.
Tip Grows well in containers. *M. neglectum* spreads well but can be invasive.

Hard fern
Blechnum spicant

Plant easy-to-grow evergreen, acid-loving hard ferns in a shady border or woodland edge. The plant is made up of erect, dark-green, lance-shaped fertile fronds and arching, glossy, deeply lobed sterile fronds.
Maintenance None needed.
Tip Rather than division, this fern is propagated from spores.

Hawthorn
Crataegus laevigata 'Paul's Scarlet'

More often seen as a hedging plant, hawthorn can be grown as a tree. This variety has attractive double red flowers and glossy green foliage. Exceptionally care-free, it requires no pruning and is generally free of pests and diseases.
Flower/Fruit Showy display of large red flowers in spring, followed by red berries in autumn.
Maintenance None necessary.
Tip Make sure you have allowed your specimen enough space.

Hazel
Corylus avellana

○ – ◗   ▲ 6m   ▶ 4m   ◊

Favoured for its early spring catkins, attractive leaf shape and autumn colour, hazel is perhaps best known for its edible nuts. This hardy shrub is easy to grow in a wide range of conditions including shade. It will grow into a small tree, or it can be pruned and used for hedging.

Flower/Fruit Clusters of pendulous yellow male catkins can be seen in late winter before the leaves. The tiny, but brilliant scarlet female flowers develop into edible nuts surrounded by green bracts.

Maintenance Trees do not normally need pruning, but hedges should be trimmed between late autumn and early spring.

Holly
Ilex species and cultivars

○ – ●   ▲ 3m   ▶ 2m   ◊

With its brilliant berries and glossy, often spiky leaves, holly is one of the most care-free of all plants. The hybrid *I.* x *meserveae* has blue-tinged foliage, best seen in the cultivars 'Blue Angel', 'Blue Prince' and 'Blue Princess'.

Flower/Fruit Insignificant white flowers followed by red berries.
Maintenance Prune to shape.
Tip Tolerates pollution.

Honeysuckle
Lonicera periclymenum

○ – ●   ▲ 6m   ▶ 3m   ◊

This honeysuckle, also known as woodbine, will vigorously scramble over supports. Its flowers are sweetly scented.

Flower Creamy white flowers from early summer to early autumn.
Maintenance Thin after flowering.
Tip They do best with their roots in shade and their shoots in the sun.

Hornbeam
Carpinus betulus

○ – ◑   ▲ 6m   ▶ 3m   ◊

This conical upright deciduous tree makes a fine hedging plant, its leafy branches withstanding severe clipping. The dark green leaves are finely toothed and give a good display of yellow in autumn.

Flower/Fruit Green catkins in spring. Tassels of seeds in autumn.

Maintenance Clip hedges in mid summer – if left unpruned, plants can grow to a height of 20m.

Hosta
Hosta species and cultivars

Hostas are grown for their sumptuous architectural heart-shaped foliage. Leaf colour varies through dusky blue-green to dark green and can be variegated and edged with different shades of cream, white, green and yellow.

Flower Lavender flowers are carried on upright stems above the leaves in early to mid summer.

Maintenance Mulch in autumn and keep well watered.

Tip Slugs and snails can be a problem; growing hostas in containers raised off the ground can help.

Houseleek
Sempervivum cultivars

All the plants in this genus of evergreen succulents are well suited to the rockery. They are mostly grown for their dense rosettes of fleshy leaves, often flushed with shades of purple or pink. The rosettes die after flowering but are constantly replaced by new rosettes.

Flower Sprays of small, starry, pink, red or white flowers appear above the foliage during summer.

Maintenance Plant ready-rooted offsets in spring or summer.

Ivy
Hedera helix

The profuse, evergreen foliage of ivy provides year-round cover. The plant is self supporting and will readily spread across walls, fences and pergolas. It is especially useful for shady places. The species has dark green leaves, but more colourful varieties are available. They include 'Caecilia' (creamy yellow and green leaves) and 'Eva' (grey-green and cream leaves) among many others.

Flower Clusters of small yellow flowers appear in autumn.

Maintenance Trim to control growth; restrict heavy pruning to spring.

Tip The late flowers of ivy will attract wildlife into the garden when there is little else in bloom.

Japanese maple
Acer japonicum

○ – ◗   ▲ 2–5m   ▶ 2–5m   ◐

The finely cut foliage of Japanese maple is attractive in spring and summer and in autumn produces a spectacular fiery display. These slow-growing deciduous trees need little attention and make an ideal focal point for a small garden.

Flower/Fruit Pale yellow or green flower clusters in spring. Red or green winged seeds in autumn.

Maintenance No pruning is necessary.

Tip Autumnal foliage ranges from fiery yellows and oranges to crimson.

Jasmine
Jasminum officinale

○ – ◗   ▲ 9m   ▶ 3m   ◐

Trained around a pergola or patio, summer jasmine is a delight, with its highly perfumed flowers. Plant in full sun, to make the scent even more intense. In warm, sheltered sites, the variegated foliage of 'Argenteovariegatum' lasts well into autumn.

Flower Fragrant clusters of white flowers appear from mid summer to early autumn.

Maintenance Thin out after flowering.

Tip Cut back *J. officinale* hard and regularly and it will form a self-supporting bush.

Kerria
Kerria japonica

○ – ◗   ▲ 2m   ▶ 2m   ○

A very easy-going shrub, kerria is a member of the rose family. Plant it and then just sit back and enjoy a golden burst of colour every spring.

Flower An abundance of yellow blooms appear from mid to late spring. Some cultivars, such as 'Pleniflora' have profuse double flowers.

Maintenance Pruning is only required to maintain a particular size.

Tip The slender arching stems can be trained up a trellis or fence.

Knotweed

Persicaria affinis

Flowers in shades of pink and red appear late in the season on this hardy herbaceous perennial. The dark green leaves, which turn to shades of red and bronze in the autumn, form low ground cover.

Flower Dense, upright spikes of small pink or red flowers appear in late summer, often persisting through autumn into winter.

Maintenance Knotweed needs little attention, but spreads rapidly once established and for this reason may be more care-free in a wild, informal scheme.

Tip Will tolerate dry situations so is suitable for a rock garden or as edging to a path.

Lady's mantle

Alchemilla mollis

Fluffy yellowish-green flowers are seen above a low mound of silky green foliage in summer. The softly hairy, almost circular leaves have shallow lobes and serrated edges.

Flower Sprays of yellowy green flowers appear in summer and last for weeks, gradually turning brown.

Maintenance Divide in autumn or spring. Seeds itself freely.

Tip The flower sprays are good for cutting and drying.

Lamb's ears

Stachys byzantina

Thick, woolly, silver grey leaves make this mat-forming perennial (above) a popular choice. In a sunny spot it can be left to cover the ground in a dense carpet.

Flower Whorls of tiny mauve-pink flowers are carried on leafy spikes above the foliage in summer.

Maintenance None needed.

Tip 'Silver Carpet' is a particularly attractive variety and 'Primrose Heron' has unusual yellow-tinged furry grey leaves.

Lawson cypress

Chamaecyparis lawsoniana

If you want a hedge in a hurry, the vigorous Lawson cyprus is a good choice since it gains 60cm in height every year. It may be too large for most gardens, but there are many smaller cultivars available.

Flower/Fruit Tiny female flowers form globular cones.

Maintenance No pruning needed.

Tip When choosing a cultivar take into account its mature height and the size of your garden.

Lettuce

Lactuca sativa cultivars

○   ▲ 15cm   ◑

There are four types of lettuce: butterhead, crisphead, cos and loose-leaf. All have varieties that are sown outdoors for a summer crop. Some loose-leaf varieties are decorative enough to be used along border edges in the garden.

Maintenance Sow seeds outdoors in late March to July. Sow in short rows every two or three weeks to give a continual supply that does not mature all at once.

Harvest From June to October. With the loose-leaf varieties, take leaves as required or cut each plant at the base after six weeks and allow it to regrow.

Lungwort

Pulmonaria saccharata

◗–●   ▲ 30cm   ▶ 30cm   ◑

Give them a shady, humus-rich spot and lungworts will reward you with attractive white-speckled foliage and charming

flowers. In borders or woodland edges they mix particularly well with primroses (*Primula vulgaris*) and hostas.

Flower Pale reddish-violet flowers appear from early to late spring.

Maintenance Divide in late autumn.

Tip Recommended cultivars include 'Frühlingshimmel' (brightly spotted leaves, pale blue flowers), 'Mrs Moon' (spotted pale green leaves, pink to violet flowers) and 'Pink Dawn' (wavy edged leaves blotched with pale green, large pink flowers).

Magnolia

Magnolia species and cultivars

○   ▲ 3–20m   ▶ 3–18m   ◑

Among the first plants to bloom in spring are the elegant magnolias, whose abundant, large and often deliciously scented flowers usually open before the leaves. They are easy to care for, requiring merely a tidy in late summer.

Flower Goblet-shaped flowers are seen in mid spring; there may be a second flush in late summer.

Maintenance Tidy up in late summer. Hard prune only mature specimens in spring.

Tip Does not flower until five years old, so buy a mature specimen. Some magnolias can grow into quite tall trees; however, there are many suitable smaller varieties.

Meadow rue

Thalictrum species and cultivars

In summer a fuzzy aerial haze of flowers can be seen above lacy grey-green foliage. *Thalictrum* is a fairly tall plant that suits the back of a border or a woodland edge.

Flower Fluffy pink sprays of flowers appear in mid summer.

Maintenance Divide clumps and replant in early spring.

Tip The stems are sturdy and do not require staking. The blossoms make excellent cut flowers and the finely divided foliage is also useful for flower arrangements.

Michaelmas daisy

Aster novi-belgii cultivars

Brightly coloured daisy flowers are held in branched sprays, often pyramid-shaped, on erect, branched, leafy stems. There are numerous cultivars available, giving a choice of colour from white to deep pink or lavender blue.

Flower Sprays of daisy-like flowers in late summer to autumn.

Maintenance Divide each spring.

Tip Recommended cultivars include 'Albanian' (white), 'Helen Ballard' (purple-red) and 'Rufus' (purple-red) and the dwarf (30cm tall), bushy cultivars of 'Chatterbox' (pale pink) and 'Lady in Blue' (lavender-blue).

Miscanthus

Miscanthus sinensis

The arching, slender, bluish-green leaves of this clump-forming perennial have silver midribs. From summer onwards it has the added interest of long-lasting, purple-silver plumes of flowers.

Flower Purple-silver feathery panicles appear from mid summer and last well into the winter.

Maintenance Divide during late spring or early summer.

Tip Other worthwhile varieties include 'Silberfeder' (silver to pinkish-brown panicles) and 'Variegatus' (leaves striped with creamy white and pale green).

Montbretia

Crocosmia cultivars

The montbretias quickly form large clumps and are ideal among shrubs. Their bright green, sword-like leaves form an attractive backdrop to the boldly coloured flowers.

hardy annual in Britain that is best grown in a sunny, sheltered spot.

Flower Cheerful trumpet-shaped blooms appear in summer and autumn. They are very short-lived.

Maintenance Sow in mid spring directly where it is to grow.

Tip These make charming conservatory plants.

Mullein

Verbascum bombyciferum

○　▲ 1.8m　▶ 80cm　◌

Showy spires of saucer-shaped flowers are produced by the compact evergreen, Verbascum. The leaves and stems are covered in dense white hairs, giving the plant an attractive silvery appearance.

Flower Spikes of sulphur yellow flowers are borne from early summer to autumn.

Maintenance Propagate by taking root cuttings during late winter.

Tip Regular deadheading will prolong the flowering period.

There are numerous cultivars to choose from.

Flower Yellow, orange or red flowers appear from late summer to early autumn.

Maintenance Between April and May plant corms 10cm deep and 20–35cm apart. Montbretias dislike long periods of frost, so a winter mulch is advisable in cold areas.

Tip Recommended cultivars include 'Canary Bird' (yellow flowers), 'Jackanapes' (flowers with yellow and dark orange petals) and 'Spitfire' (fiery orange flowers).

Morning glory

Ipomoea purpurea

○　▲ 5m　▶ 1.5m　◑

Morning glory is grown for its abundantly produced trumpet-shaped flowers that may be red, purple, white or striped. It is a half-

Nasturtium

Tropaeolum majus

○ ▲ 2m ▶ 2.3m ◐

This tender annual has a variety of uses. Its richly coloured trumpet-shaped blooms brighten up borders, trellises, pots and hanging baskets. It does best in poor soil, where it will flower profusely. The circular leaves are also attractive.

Flower Yellow, orange or red flowers appear in summer.

Maintenance None needed.

Tip Plants in the 'Alaska Series' have cream-and-green variegated foliage and orange or red flowers; 'Hermine Grashoff' has double orange-scarlet flowers.

Oregon grape

Mahonia aquifolium

○ – ● ▲ 2m ▶ 2m ◌

With its glossy dark green leaves and golden yellow, sweetly scented flowers, mahonia brightens up the garden in winter and spring. Some varieties such as

'Atropurpurea' have reddish purple leaves.

Flower/Fruit Bright yellow flowers in mid to late spring are followed by small grape-like berries, hence the common name.

Maintenance No pruning needed except to remove any suckers.

Tip *M. aquifolium* is often grown as ground cover or as a low hedge.

Pachysandra

Pachysandra terminalis

◗ – ● ▲ 30cm ▶ 50cm ◐

Another hardy, evergreen ground-cover plant for shady places. It spreads easily by means of creeping roots, forming a carpet of rich green leathery leaves. White flowers are dotted among the foliage in spring.

Flower Spikes of white flowers appear in late and early spring.

Maintenance None necessary.

Tip A useful choice for growing at the foot of shade-loving shrubs such as rhododendrons and camellias.

Pelargonium

Pelargonium cultivars

○ – ◗ ▲ 60cm ▶ 30cm ◐

The robust pelargoniums offer a huge variety of flower colour and handsome foliage. They are easy to grow and their ability to withstand some drought means that they can survive the odd lapse in watering. There are four groups: 'ivy-leaved' with a trailing habit for hanging baskets;

Maintenance None, except to control the size of plants.

Tip Useful under deciduous trees and shrubs and in wild gardens.

'regal' with large, richly coloured flowers; 'scented-leaved' with pleasantly aromatic foliage; and 'zonal' where the leaves are marked with a band of contrasting colour. All can be grown in containers or used in bedding schemes.

Flower Five-petalled flowers in shades of pink, purple, red, white and bicoloured appear from early to late summer.

Maintenance Deadhead to extend the flowering period. Repot in spring and replace every two years. Replace bedding plants annually.

Periwinkle
Vinca major

Vigorous creeping periwinkles form extensive carpets of foliage in any location as long as the soil is not too dry. Thriving in partial or full shade, they will spread indefinitely, bearing masses of blue flowers.

Flower Blue, five-petalled flowers appear in spring and early summer. *V. major* var. *alba* has white flowers and var. *oxyloba* produces dark violet flowers.

Pine
Pinus mugo

A hardy, slow-growing evergreen that bears red female flowers among its densely packed long, dark-green needles. May form a large shrubby bush or a small tree. It is a good maintenance-free choice for awkward places.

Flower/Fruit Red female flowers, green male flowers. Blackish-brown cones ripen to yellow-brown.

Maintenance Remove spindly branches.

Tip Grow in acid soil.

Pot marigold

Calendula officinalis

○	▲ 60cm	▶ 25cm	◊

The daisy-like flowers of these fast-growing annuals can be relied upon to bring a burst of colour to a bed or border the whole summer long. The flowers peep out among thick, aromatic pale green foliage. There are numerous cultivated varieties to choose from with semi-double and double flowers.

Flower Yellow, orange, apricot or cream flowers are borne from late spring through to late summer.
Maintenance None needed.
Tip Deadhead regularly to encourage a continuous show of flowers.

Privet

Ligustrum vulgare

○–●	▲ 5m	▶ 3m	◑

Privet is a traditional choice for hedges, being hardy, fast-growing and able to withstand hard pruning. Common privet has mid-green foliage, but there are golden or variegated varieties available.
Flower/Fruit White flower clusters appear from early to mid summer followed by shiny black autumn fruits.
Maintenance Prune hedges to desired shape in mid summer.
Tip Birds are attracted to the fruits.

Purple loosestrife

Lythrum salicaria

○–◗	▲ 1.5m	▶ 1m	●

Slender wands of reddish purple flowers distinguish this upright, hardy perennial. The tubular-based flowers are carried on square stems above lance-shaped leaves that may turn yellow in autumn. It thrives in the boggy soil found at water margins, but can easily be grown elsewhere in the garden on rich moisture-retentive soil.
Flower Spikes of reddish-purple flowers appear in mid summer.
Maintenance Divide overcrowded clumps in autumn or spring.
Tip Deadhead to prevent the spread of self-sown seed.

Radish
Raphanus sativus cultivars

Quick and easy to grow, radishes come in different colours and sizes. Summer salad varieties may be red, red and white or white, and either spherical or cylindrical.
Maintenance Sow outdoors in March to July every two weeks for a continual supply. Sow thinly in drills and thin if necessary soon after seedlings emerge. Rows should be 15cm apart.
Harvest When young – three to six weeks after sowing.
Tip There are winter radish varieties for harvesting later in the season. Sow them in late July and August for a crop 10 or 12 weeks later.

Raspberry
Rubus idaeus

Raspberries are an easy and very rewarding crop. The tall upright canes require staking and a yearly prune, but the reward is an abundance of sweet juicy fruit year after year. Since they flower in early summer, frost damage is rare and the plants thrive in typically cool, wet British summers.
Flower Clusters of white flowers in summer.
Maintenance In autumn, after harvesting, cut those canes that have borne fruit back to soil level. Tie new canes to wires for fruit next year.
Harvest Mid summer to mid autumn, depending on the variety.
Tip Choose 'Glen Moy' for early fruit and 'Autumn Bliss' for a later harvest.

Rodgersia
Rodgersia pinnata

Large, divided leaves, held on tall stalks give rodgersias architectural value in the garden.

The handsome flowers are held in plumes above the foliage in summer. They do well when sited in boggy ground beside ponds and streams.
Flower Plumes of tiny star-like flowers, in shades of white, yellow or pink, appear in mid summer.
Maintenance Divide rhizomes in either spring or autumn.
Tip Recommended cultivars include 'Elegans' (cream flowers) and 'Superba' (rose-pink flowers).

ROSES

Climbing and rambling roses

Climbing roses provide a maximum of flowers in a minimum of space. Scrambling over house walls, pergolas or arches, they add a romantic touch to your garden. Climbers can reach a height of up to 4m, and the arching shoots of ramblers can grow longer than that.

Flower All colours except blue and black, single to fully double, some scented. Climbers are mostly repeat flowering, while most ramblers flower once,

Maintenance Train side shoots horizontally to promote flowering; if necessary, thin out in spring.

Tip Best climbers include 'New Dawn' (mother-of-pearl coloured), and 'Compassion' (fragrant, salmon-pink). Best ramblers include 'Super Excelsa' (carmine pink, double, repeat flowering).

English roses

English roses, developed by the rose breeder David Austin, combine the achievements of modern breeding – repeat flowering, good health and modern colours – with the beauty and scent of older rose varieties. In addition, they are considered robust and fast-growing.

Flower All colours except blue and black, usually scented. Flowers once or repeatedly, depending on cultivar.

Maintenance If not pruned back in spring, these roses will flower earlier; if pruned back, they become sturdier. Deadheading can encourage repeat flowering.

Tip 'Abraham Darby', apricot to pink in colour, is an especially bewitching and robust variety.

Ground-cover roses

○ – ◑　▲ 1.5m　▶ 3m　◐

With their low-growing arched shoots, ground-cover roses create a carpet of flowers. They look most attractive when allowed to tumble over a wall or sprawl down a bank.

Flower Pink, white, yellow or red.

Maintenance They do not usually need pruning, but can be cut back hard if necessary; do not prune varieties growing on their own rootstock by more than a few inches every few years.

Tip Robust varieties, which also do well in semi-shade, include 'The Fairy' (pink, double), and 'Surrey' (clusters of pink flowers). 'Kent' (white, slightly double) is scented, flowers in summer, and has glossy foliage. All three repeat flower.

Gallica roses

Rosa gallica cultivars

○ – ◑　▲ 3m　▶ 2m　◐

The robust, thorny *R. gallica* also known as the Apothecary's rose, is the original red rose of Lancaster and has been cultivated for more than 500 years. It flowers once a year in summer.

Flower/Fruit Large, deep pink blooms appear in June and turn into rounded hips.

Maintenance Thin if needed, can also be pruned back radically.

Tip There are numerous varieties available, for example 'Versicolor' (pale pink blooms, striped and splashed with reddish pink), also known as *R. mundi*.

Modern shrub roses

○ – ◑　▲ 2m　▶ 2m　◐

With these slightly taller shrubs, you can admire their abundant flowers well into the autumn. They are good as specimen plants or to form loose hedges and also make ideal plants for smaller gardens.

Flower/Fruit All colours except blue and black, often scented; also bears attractive red to black hips.

Maintenance Deadhead to encourage repeat flowering; cut out dead stems in the spring.

Tip Robust varieties include 'Mozart' (pink centres, carmine outside, single) and 'Westerland' (orange-pink).

Rugosa roses

Rosa rugosa cultivars

○ – ◑　▲ 2m　▶ 1.5m　○

The many descendants of *R. rugosa* are robust and will grow in almost any soil. They are vigorous and colourful border plants and can be grown into a superb hedge with their prickly shoots quickly forming a dense, leafy thicket.

Flower/Fruit White, yellow, pink, red, single to semidouble, scented flowers; also produces large brightly coloured hips that last well into the winter.

Maintenance Can be pruned back hard, according to need.

Tip Lime-rich soil will turn its leaves yellow. It can tolerate dry and even slightly salty soils.

Rowan

Sorbus aucuparia

Autumn berries and graceful foliage earn the easily grown deciduous rowan a place in most gardens. The pinnate leaves give rich coppery tones in autumn and the brilliant red berries are always plentiful. When grown as trees they require no pruning and are generally free of pests and diseases.

Flower/Fruit Clusters of white, scented flowers borne in late spring followed by bright red berries.

Maintenance No pruning needed.

Tip The autumn berries are adored by birds and will attract them into your garden.

Rudbeckia

Rudbeckia species and cultivars

The sturdy golden flowerheads of rudbeckia give a reliable display year after year. The prominent cone-shaped centre is black, surrounded by gracefully drooping petals. Allow room for new plants to spread and form clumps.

Flower Golden yellow single flowers with black centres appear during late summer to early autumn.

Maintenance Divide in spring or autumn. Deadhead to prolong flowering.

Tip Apply a mulch around the base of plants in spring to prevent flowering plants from wilting in hot sun.

Sage

Salvia officinalis Purpurascens Group

Sage is an aromatic herb widely grown for its ornamental foliage as well as for its use in cooking. It is tough and tolerant of poor, dry soil. This particular variety has attractive soft, purple leaves that darken through the summer.

Flower Short spikes of purple flowers appear intermittently on plants throughout the summer.

Maintenance Control the size of mature plants by cutting back in spring.

Tip Cutting back flowering stems encourages a second crop of blooms later in the season.

St John's wort

Hypericum calycinum

Hypericums are vigorous, hardy plants that readily suppress weeds. This species, also known as rose of Sharon, spreads rapidly and will even grow in deep shade. It has a tough, creeping rootstock, so can be somewhat invasive.

Flower Bright yellow flowers are borne throughout the summer.
Maintenance Prune back hard each spring.
Tip Plants bear plenty of highly decorative berries in autumn.

Sensitive fern
Onoclea sensibilis

◗–● ▲ 60cm ▶ 60cm ◉

This moisture-loving fern produces triangular, pink-bronze, erect fronds that later become mid green and arching. The pinnate sterile fronds die back with the first frost while the more persistent bipinnate fertile fronds turn dark brown. Massed together these plants can create a striking winter display.
Maintenance Divide in spring.

Shrub verbena
Lantana camara

○ ▲ 2.5m ▶ 1.3m ◑

Grow this tender evergreen shrub in a greenhouse or conservatory, or in tubs for a summer display. It produces large heads of flowers, sometimes with different colours appearing on the same plant. The oval, mid green leaves often have a pungent aroma.

Flower Rounded heads of tiny flowers in shades of yellow, orange or red appear throughout the summer.
Maintenance Trim back weak or dead shoots in spring. Outdoor specimens can be overwintered in a cool greenhouse.
Tip A recommended cultivar is 'Brasier' with bright red flowers.

Siberian iris
Iris sibirica

○–◗ ▲ 1m ▶ 1m ◉

Named for the Greek goddess of the rainbow, iris flowers combine an architectural flower form with a huge range of rich colours. This beardless water iris does well on the margins of ponds or streams but dislikes waterlogging.
Flower Up to five flowers, which vary from white to blue, are borne in early summer.
Maintenance Divide rhizomes after flowering every three years. Replant 2.5cm deep in moist soil.
Tip Irises are heavy feeders so spread compost or manure around the plants.

Smoke bush
Cotinus coggygria

◐ – ◐   ▲ 5m   ▶ 4m   ◌

Plant the hardy deciduous smoke bush among green plants where its red and yellow autumn foliage will create an attractive contrast. The shrubs also make striking free-standing specimens with their rounded, spreading habit.

Flower Profuse plumes of tiny fawn flowers are displayed during mid summer, turning grey later.

Maintenance Pruning not needed except to clear dead wood in spring.

Tip The leaves do not colour as well on rich, manured soils.

Spindle tree
Euonymus fortunei 'Emerald Gaiety'

◐ – ●   ▲ 1m   ▶ 1.5m   ◔

With eye-catching, creamy white-edged leaves that turn an attractive bronze colour in winter, 'Emerald Gaiety' has year-round value in the garden. A dense, hardy evergreen, its compact height and spread make it a useful ground-cover plant.

Flower/Fruit Insignificant flowers; rarely produces berries.

Maintenance Pruning is not required except to keep plants within their allotted space. Do this any time except spring.

Spiraea
Spiraea japonica

◐ – ◑   ▲ 1.5m   ▶ 1.2m   ◔

They are deciduous, but the dense growth of hardy spireas make them ideal as hedging plants. *S. japonica* is a medium-sized shrub that bears large rosy pink flowerheads in summer. There are various cultivars available for both flowers and foliage in different colours.

Flower Rosy pink flattish clusters in mid to late summer.

Maintenance Cut back previous year's growth to 15cm above ground during the second season. Thereafter shear to shape after flowering.

Spotted laurel
Aucuba japonica

◐ – ◑   ▲ 3m   ▶ 3m   ◌

Glossy, deep-green, oval leaves give permanent value to the sturdy evergreen laurel. It is easy to grow, frost hardy and tolerates pollution. With a bushy, upright habit it can be planted in rows to create a formal hedge or screen. 'Crotonifolia' is an attractive variegated variety.

Flower/Fruit Small male and female flowers appear on different plants. Vivid red oval berries follow on fertilised female plants.

Maintenance Trim hedges during the growing season to maintain the desired shape of a plant.

Tip Plant male and female plants to ensure a good show of berries.

Spruce

Picea pungens 'Globosa'

○ – ◑   ▲ 80cm   ▶ 80cm   ◌

It may be hard to imagine a low-growing spruce, but this variety forms a flattened dome just 80cm high and wide. Its vivid blue needles bring colour to mixed borders and rockeries all year round.

Flower/Fruit Red and green flowers are followed by egg-shaped, pale brown cones.

Maintenance Confine any pruning to removing damaged branches. Do this during winter to avoid resin bleeding, which can attract disease.

Tip The aromatic long-lasting foliage is good for decorations and flower arrangements.

Spurge

Euphorbia myrsinites

○   ▲ 20cm   ▶ 40cm   ◌

A low-growing biennial with leafy prostrate stems emerging from a woody crown. The yellowy green flowerheads are carried on the previous season's shoots. The thick blue-grey leaves spiral attractively around the stems.

Flower Yellowy green flowerheads appear from late winter to mid spring. Yellowy bracts may change to orange-yellow during the summer.

Maintenance Cut back flowering shoots to ground level in late summer and leave current season's shoots (which will flower the following year).

Tip The milky white sap is toxic and so euphorbias should not be planted near a fishpond; avoid skin contact.

Stonecrop

Sedum 'Herbstfreude'

○ – ◑   ▲ 45cm   ▶ 45cm   ◌

Sedums are easy to grow. Most prefer dry, hot, sunny locations, but this cultivar prefers partial shade. Its attractive pink flowerheads deepen to bronze red. Stout, upright stems bear pale green, fleshy, oval-shaped leaves with toothed edges.

Flower Pink to bronze-red flowers in early and mid summer.

Maintenance Divide in late autumn. Leave dead growth in place over winter, clearing it away in early spring.

Strawberry

Fragaria x ananassa

Quick to produce a harvest, and compact enough for the smallest garden – it can even be grown in containers – the strawberry is a most desirable fruit. Grow several varieties to prolong the fruiting season.

Flower Starry white flowers in late spring and summer.

Maintenance Protect flowers from late spring frosts with straw or fleece. As fruits grow, protect from soil splash by tucking straw under them.

Harvest From early to late summer, depending on variety.

Tip After harvest cut back foliage to 10cm from the crown; remove it and burn with any straw and debris.

Sunflower

Helianthus atrorubens

Despite their name, sunflowers do well in partial shade as well as full sun. This species is a perennial and positioned at the back of

a border or against a wall, it will produce large flowers on tall stems year after year.

Flower Orange-yellow flowers with maroon centres are borne from late summer through to early autumn.

Maintenance Can be invasive; curtail spread by lifting and replanting in spring.

Tip The seed heads encourage finches into the garden in autumn.

Switch grass

Panicum virgatum 'Rubrum'

Switch grass makes good-sized clumps of medium height. In autumn it produces sprays of tiny flowers and the foliage ripens to a rich reddish colour.

Flower Panicles of tiny green spikelets appear in late summer.

Maintenance Divide clumps any time of year except summer.

Tip Use this stunning grass as a focal point.

Tagetes

Tagetes species and cultivars

Crisp flowers in a range of bright yellow, orange and red shades are borne in profusion during the summer months. There are few bedding plants that can rival tagetes in terms of ease of cultivation and length of flowering. The genus includes French and African marigolds – *T. patula* and *T. erecta* respectively – admired for their golden double blooms. *T. tenuifolia* produces masses of small, single flowers in a range of bright colours. It has a very bushy habit and the blooms appear in such profusion that the plant can look like a ball of flowers. Tagetes are often grown to great effect at the front of a border and do best in full sun.

Flower Yellow, orange, red or russet flowers are borne throughout the summer.

Maintenance Water thoroughly during prolonged dry spells.

Tip *T. patula* 'Safari Tangerine' (above) has orange-yellow, semi-double flowers.

Tickseed
Bidens ferulifolia

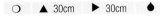
○ ▲ 30cm ▶ 30cm ●

With a naturally spreading, thin stemmed habit, tickseed drapes prettily out of a hanging basket or container. In the summer the stems are covered in yellow flowers.
Flower Yellow flowers bloom from early summer to early autumn.
Maintenance Too tender to survive outdoors after the first frost, but can be overwintered in a cool greenhouse.
Tip Though it prefers full sun, it will grow in light shade.

Tulip
Tulipa species and cultivars

○ – ◗ ▲ 40cm ▶ 30cm ◐

This is another bulb that has been bred into thousands of colours and forms. For example, the double early tulips have showy double blooms, while the Greigii tulips offer attractive foliage, their leaves marked with

maroon mottling. The flowers are generally goblet shaped and the leaves are bright green and broadly lance shaped.
Flower Every conceivable colour except true blue, in late spring.
Maintenance In autumn plant bulbs 10–15cm deep at 10cm intervals.
Tip Tulips are a popular choice for growing in containers.

Viburnum
Viburnum davidii

○ – ◗ ▲ 1.5m ▶ 2m ◐

Viburnum is easily grown and suitable for almost every location. This species is a low-growing, round-headed evergreen with leathery, dark green, veined leaves. It is an undemanding plant that makes a handsome addition to the back of a border.
Flower/Fruit Flat clusters of small white flowers are borne in early summer. The iridescent blue fruits last through winter.
Maintenance Prune immediately after the plant has flowered.
Tip Large-leaved viburnums do not tolerate wind exposure. For a good show of berries, plant in groups of two or three.

Water lily

Nymphaea cultivars

Grown for their waxy, star or cup-shaped summer flowers and floating foliage, water lilies are deciduous, perennial aquatic plants. The leaves shade the surface of the water and so help to reduce the amount of algae in a pond. There are varieties to suit every pond depth, including miniature varieties for planting in water tubs.

Flower White, pink, red, yellow or orange flowers open in summer.

Maintenance To avoid congestion, divide every three to five years.

Tip Recommended cultivars include 'Gonnère' (double white flowers) and 'Fabiola' (rose-pink flowers flushed red at the base).

Windflower

Anemone hupehensis var. *japonica*

Plant this spreading herbaceous perennial in dappled shade for a late show of flowers that will last into the autumn.

Flower Clusters of clear pink flowers appear from late summer to mid autumn.

Maintenance Plant in spring or early summer. Mulch during the hotter months.

Tip When planting out add plenty of humus to the soil.

Witch hazel

Hamamelis species and cultivars

When the rest of the garden is bare, the witch hazel can be relied upon to bring a burst of colour. Clusters of spidery flowers appear in profusion during mid winter, surviving the harshest frosts. The trees also have colourful autumn foliage.

Flower Small yellow, red or orange flowers with a strong scent appear in mid winter.

Maintenance Remove any dead wood in autumn and winter.

Tip Although they are slow growing, witch hazels can grow to become as broad as they are tall and deserve to be given ample space in the garden.

Yarrow

Achillea millefolium

Brightly coloured summer flowers and ferny, greyish-green foliage make these herbaceous evergreen perennials a popular choice for sunny borders and beds.

Flower Flat heads of white or pink flowers appear in summer.

Maintenance Lift and divide plants every three years.

Tip Colourful varieties include 'Lilac Beauty' (light mauve flowers) and 'Paprika' (orange-red and yellow flowers).

© RD = Reader's Digest Association, MW=Mark Winwood, DP=Debbie Patterson
All artwork=© Reader's Digest Association

T=Top, B=Bottom, L=Left, R=Right, C=Centre

Cover Top Gap Photos Ltd/Jerry Harpur **Cover Centre** iStockphoto.com/Lise Gagne **Cover Bottom** iStockphoto.com/Terry Wilson **1** ShutterStock, Inc/Malibu Books **2–3** ShutterStock, Inc/Gillian Mowbray **4–5** iStockphoto.com/Fenghua He **5 TR** iStockphoto.com/Nicolas Loran **BR** iStockphoto.com/Vera Bogaerts **6** iStockphoto.com/deetone **8–9** iStockphoto.com/Nicolas Loran **11** Brigitte Kleinod **13** Photolibrary Group/ Friedrich Strauss **14** Wolfgang Redeleit **16 L** Reinhard-Tierfoto **R** Wolfgang Redeleit **18 T** Gardena AG **B** The Garden Collection/Andrew Lawson **19** iStockphoto.com/Johanna Goodyear **20 L** iStockphoto.com/Luca Manieri **C** iStockphoto.com/Eric Naud **R** © RD/MW **21 L** iStockphoto.com/Andreas Kaspar **C** iStockphoto.com/ Joshua Northrup **R** iStockphoto.com/ Webphotographeer **22 L** iStockphoto.com/Luca Manieri **C** iStockphoto.com/ Eric Naud **R** © RD/MW **23 L** iStockphoto.com/Andreas Kaspar **C** iStockphoto.com/Josuha Northrup **R** iStockphoto.com/ Webphotographeer **24–25** iStockphoto.com/Fenghua He **26** Photolibrary Group/Friedrich Strauss **27** Reinhard-Tierfoto **29** Reinhard-Tierfoto **30** Wolfgang Redeleit **31** © RD **33** Reinhard-Tierfoto **34** Reinhard-Tierfoto **36** iStockphoto.com/lubilub **37 B** Wolfgang Redeleit **38** Reinhard-Tierfoto **39** ShutterStock, Inc/Denise Kappa **40** Friedrich Strauss **42** Friedrich Strauss **45 L** Wolfgang Redeleit **47** Friedrich Strauss **50** Eltima Fertighecken **53** © RD/DP **55** Friedrich Strauss **57** © RD/DP **58** © RD/DP **61** iStockphoto.com/YinYang **62** © RD/DP **66** Friedrich Strauss **67 B** Wolfgang Redeleit **68 B** iStockphoto.com/Valentin Casarsa **69 TR** Photolibrary Group/Mark Winwood **BR** Wolfgang Redeleit **70 L** Gardena AG **R** Wolfgang Redeleit **71 T** Photolibrary Group/Friedrich Strauss **CR** Wolfgang Redeleit **72** Reinhard-Tierfoto **74** Reinhard-Tierfoto **75** Reinhard-Tierfoto **78** © RD/DP **80** Reinhard-Tierfoto **81 TL** iStockphoto.com/Timo Newton-Syms **82 L** iStockphoto.com/Dominique Rodrigue **R** iStockphoto.com/Amber Tulissi **83** Gardena AG **84** iStockphoto.com/Guy Nicholls **85 T** Wolfgang Redeleit **86** iStockphoto.com/Neil Wigmore **87** © RD/DP **88 B** Brigitte & Siegfried Stein **90–91** iStockphoto.com/Vera Bogaerts **92 L** © RD **R** IFB München **93** © RD **94 L** Photolibrary Group/ Mayer/Le Scanff **R** © RD **95–124** © RD

Reader's Digest The Easy-care Garden is based on material in *The Time-saving Garden* and *New Encyclopedia of Garden Plants & Flowers*, all published by The Reader's Digest Association Limited, London.

First Edition Copyright © 2008

The Reader's Digest Association Limited, 11 Westferry Circus, Canary Wharf, London E14 4HE **www.readersdigest.co.uk**

Editors Caroline Smith, Helen Spence
Art Editor Jane McKenna
Proofreader Rosemary Wighton
Indexer Hilary Bird
Picture Researcher Rosie Taylor

Reader's Digest General Books
Editorial Director Julian Browne
Art Director Anne-Marie Bulat
Managing Editor Nina Hathway
Head of Book Development Sarah Bloxham
Picture Resource Manager Sarah Stewart-Richardson
Pre-press Account Manager Dean Russell
Production Controller Sandra Fuller
Product Production Manager Claudette Bramble

Origination Colour Systems Limited, London
Printed in China

All rights reserved.

No part of this book may be reproduced, stored in a retrieval system or transmitted in any form or by any means, electronic, electrostatic, magnetic tape, mechanical, photocopying, recording or otherwise, without permission in writing from the publishers.

® Reader's Digest, The Digest and the Pegasus logo are registered trademarks of The Reader's Digest Association, Inc., of Pleasantville, New York, USA

We are committed both to the quality of our products and the service we provide to our customers. We value your comments, so please do contact us on **08705 113366** or via our website at **www.readersdigest.co.uk**

If you have any comments or suggestions about the content of our books, email us at **gbeditorial@readersdigest.co.uk**

ISBN 978 0 276 44274 2
BOOK CODE 400-370 UP0000-1
ORACLE CODE 250011975H.00.24